Physical Characteris... Cane Cors...

(from the Fédération Cynologique Internationale breed standard)

Body: Compact, strong and very muscular.

Back: Wide, very muscular as the whole upper line of the trunk.

Tail: Inserted quite high on the rump line, thick at the root and not too tapering at the tip.

Hindquarters: Perpendicular, seen from the front or in profile. Well proportioned to the size of the dog, strong and powerful.

Height at the withers: For males from 64 cm to 68 cm. For females from 60 cm to 64 cm. With allowance of ±2 cm.

Color: Black, plum-gray, slate, light gray, light fawn, deer fawn, dark fawn and tubby (very well marked stripes on different shades of fawn and gray). A small white patch on the chest, on the feet tips and on the nose bridge is accepted.

Weight: Males from 45 to 50 kg. Ratio weight/size 0.710 (kg/cm). Females from 40 to 45 kg. Ratio weight/size 0.680 (kg/cm).

Hindfeet: Of a slightly more oval shape than the fore ones and with less arched toes.

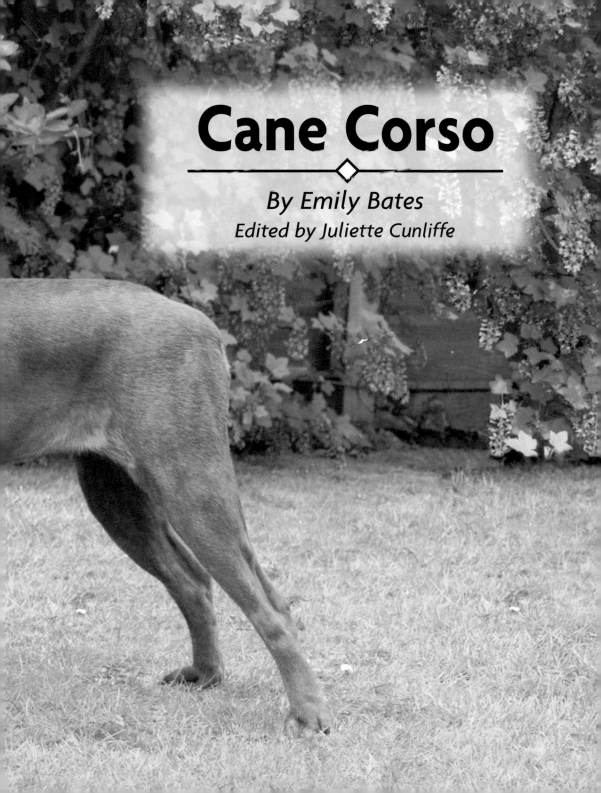

Cane Corso

By Emily Bates

Edited by Juliette Cunliffe

Contents

Training Your Cane Corso 82

By Charlotte Schwartz
Be informed about the importance of training your Cane Corso from the basics of housebreaking and understanding the development of a young dog to executing obedience commands (sit, stay, down, etc.).

Health Care of Your Cane Corso 107

Discover how to select a qualified vet and care for your dog at all stages of life. Topics include vaccinations, skin problems, dealing with external and internal parasites and common medical and behavioral conditions.

Showing Your Cane Corso 138

Enter the dog-show world and find out how shows are organized and how a champion is made. Go beyond the conformation ring to competitive trials and events. Learn about the Fédération Cynologique Internationale, the world kennel club that accepts the Cane Corso.

Behavior of Your Cane Corso 144

Learn to recognize and handle common behavioral problems in your Cane Corso, including barking, jumping up, aggression with people and other dogs, chewing, digging, separation anxiety, etc.

KENNEL CLUB BOOKS: CANE CORSO
ISBN: 1-59378-346-9

Copyright © 2004
Kennel Club Books, Inc., 308 Main Street, Allenhurst, NJ 07711 USA
Cover Design Patented: US 6,435,559 B2 • Printed in South Korea

Photography by Isabelle Français and Michael Trafford, with additional photographs by:
Norvia Behling, T. J. Calhoun, Carolina Biological Supply, Doskocil, James Hayden-Yoav, James R. Hayden, RBP, Carol Ann Johnson, Bill Jonas, Dwight R. Kuhn, Dr. Dennis Kunkel, Mikki Pet Products, Phototake, Jean Claude Revy, Dr. Andrew Spielman and Alice van Kempen.

Illustrations by Patricia Peters.

The publisher wishes to thank all of the owners of the dogs featured in this book, including Alexandra Bark, Filippo A. Barone, Sandra Freeman, Philippe Hardy, Delonte Howell, Cory and Diane Machese, Kimberly A. Seipel, Linda M. Valentine and Mark Wilson.

The Cane Corso is directly descended from Roman war dogs. Today the breed is gaining popularity outside Italy with those who want a noble canine companion and guardian of the home.

HISTORY OF THE

CANE CORSO

ORIGIN OF THE BREED

The Cane Corso, like the Neapolitan Mastiff, is directly descended from the old Roman War Dog, *Canis Pugnax*. Of these two breeds, the Cane Corso is lighter and, in the Middle Ages, was used as a huntor of wild game. This was a powerful and courageous dog whose skills were especially valuable on wild boar, although he was also used on stag, bear and other animals. Even today, Italian fanciers of the breed claim that this is "the only true coursing mastiff." He was also used as a butcher's dog, a war dog and as a gladiator in the arena. His talents have historically lain in keeping away predators of every kind; indeed, in many cases, the breed is still used as a protector.

When Rome conquered Briton, war dogs were already common all over the Middle East and Europe. Rome had *Canis Pugnax* when they conquered Briton, but they watched the British war dogs defeat their own dogs on the battlefield and raved about the superiority of the "broad-mouthed dogs of England."

Notably impressed, they imported great numbers of these dogs to Rome as gifts, and many were used to perform in the arena. It seems reasonable to assume that the Romans would have introduced these British dogs to their own lines, which could explain why the brindle color is quite prevalent in Cane Corsi. It is clear that the Neapolitan Mastiff and the Cane Corso are close cousins; indeed, until 1949 they even shared the same name. However, unlike the Neapolitan Mastiff, the Cane Corso has impressive speed and agility for such a large dog.

The Cane Corso was mentioned in early prose and there is convincing evidence that the breed was put to military use in 1137 in Monopoli di Sabina, near Rome. Kennels from this period link the breed closely with Roman history. But time moved on and, with it, the Cane's employ understandably altered.

It should be recognized that, throughout the centuries, the Cane Corso breed, through Natural Selection, maintained close contact with its environment through the roles it was required to play. For much of history, survival of any breed was dependent upon its ability to work, so the decision to raise and to maintain a breed was largely an economic one.

EARLY DAYS IN ITALY

The hunting of big game in Italy declined, but the Cane Corso still survived, for the breed found its home with Italian farmers. Farmers found the Cane to be useful as a drover, especially when moving animals to market or to the slaughter-house. The Cane Corso also was an important assistant to the butcher, for the dog would help him to block animals during the slaughtering process if necessary. If the slaughtering procedure went wrong, a bull would understandably become highly dangerous and the dog would stop the bull's aggression by biting it on the nose or lips and then forcing it to its knees.

The Cane was also useful on farms for protecting livestock from predators, both human and

Neapolitan Mastiff and (inset) head study. The Neo, as he is called, is another mastiff breed from Italy and a close relative of the Cane Corso.

Cane Corso and (inset) head study. Though bearing many similarities to the Neapolitan Mastiff, the Cane Corso possesses speed and agility that his heavier cousin does not.

those of the four-legged kind. He also seems often to have run alongside carts to protect them and their contents against highwaymen, and sometimes wealthy travelers used this breed for protection when traveling by stagecoach. Indeed the Cane soon proved himself as an admirable guard dog for home, land and livestock, and he still performs these duties in his homeland today.

The Cane, like the people of Italy, has enjoyed mixed times of splendor and misery. With the introduction of firearms bringing a change in hunting methods, coupled with the disappearance of wild game, the breed has at times seemed in danger of serious decline, particularly during a period of time starting with World War II. Nonetheless, this is an undisputedly talented breed and, thanks to these talents, is now regaining popularity at an incredible rate.

The breed has always been present in the south of Italy, most probably due to the fact that, in that region, there is an archaic agricultural system that benefits greatly from a multi-purpose dog such as the Cane Corso. The breed's behavioral characteristics relate to the work it is required to do, and the breed shows not only esthetic harmony but also an important balance in its character.

THE BREED IN MODERN-DAY ITALY

By the 1970s, there was fear for the survival of the breed in Italy. The Cane Corso was reduced to only a few typical examples despite the efforts of interested enthusiasts such as Count Bonatti and Professor Ballota. However, in 1976, Dr. Breber captured the interest not only of the dog fraternity but also of the public with an article that was published in the Italian Kennel Club's (ENCI) magazine.

With interest in the breed kindled, Dr. Breber set up a rescue mission with a group of enthusiasts that had been in contact with him since the publication of his article. In October of 1983, the Società Amatori Cane Corso (SACC) was formed but suffered a severe change three years later when Dr. Breber abandoned the society. A dog, Bresir, had been selected as the basis on which the breed standard was built. He was a son of Dauno and Tipsi, both chosen by Dr. Breber. With Dr. Breber's departure from the club, it became centered around Giancarlo Malavasi's kennels in Mantova, and the running of the relatively newly formed society was placed largely in the hands of Stafano Gandolfi, Gianantonio Sereni and Fernando Casolino.

It was now important to move the breeding program ahead at all costs, giving rise to the centralized operation of the club. Although the process may not always have been as democratic as it might have been, activities were carried out energetically and brought about results. Meetings were held, giving the breed exposure to interested parties, and tests and measurements were carried out. Such activities led to an official standard's being edited by Dr. Antonio Morisiani, and this was ratified by ENCI in 1987. There was, though, discussion as to the accuracy or otherwise of the standard, particularly with reference to the bite.

In 1992, ENCI began to record the birth of puppies whose sire and dam had been verified by judges, initially in the Libro Apperto ("Open Book"). When the breed was officially recognized on January 20, 1994, the data contained in the Libro Apperto was transferred to official records. Unfortunately, due to enthusiasm and curiosity surrounding the Cane Corso, and in the knowledge that an increase in number of litters born would help recognition, there was some decline in the overall quality of dogs produced. People were aware of this, and on May 22, 1996, the best Cane Corsi were gathered together at Arese, with Ch. Boris used as the model for presentation of the breed's characteristics. Just a few months later, in November 1996, the breed became recognized at an international level.

In 1999, ENCI relieved the SACC of recognition as the official club for the breed and the Associazione Italiana Cane Corso (AICC) was founded, with Mr. Renzo Carosio as president. The club has established close contact with America's International Cane Corso Federation (ICCF) and Holland's Cane Corso Club of the Netherlands (CCCN). Today, SACC is once again the official ENCI parent club

VITO INDIVERI'S EXPERIENCES IN ITALY'S SOUTH

Vito Indiveri's personal recollections of his experience with the breed in southern Italy make fascinating reading and provide an insight into the breed from the 1970s. Indiveri came from a family of carters and horse merchants who had always had Pomeranians and Cane Corsi. The latter were used in the barnyard to guard the horses but, with the introduction of agricultural machines, the dogs vanished. Indiveri rediscovered

NICE CATCH!

The Cane Corso is a true working breed that excels as a "catch dog." On leash, the dog is brought within sight of a boar. When he spots the boar, he is released and he makes a beeline for the boar in total silence. The catch dog then clamps down on the boar's head and when the "bay dogs" see that he has hold of the boar's head, they come to his assistance. Today the Cane Corso is still used in Italy to keep farms free of wild boar.

the breed in the late 1970s, at a farm in Aprecenia.

As a traveling salesman, he always journeyed in the countryside rather than in large cities, visiting very remote areas as far south as Sicily. He regularly found dogs owned by peasant farmers, and all were made to work. Some were used to keep tabs on sheep and some as herders to bring sheep to pasture, while others were used as hunting dogs, particularly for badger and boar, but also for porcupine and the now-extinct Italian forest cat.

Cane Corsi were never sold and there was a certain jealousy between the families that raised them. From each litter, only the useful puppies were retained, the others eliminated. A lot of inbreeding took place, but puppies were sometimes exchanged at fairs, thereby bringing in new bloodlines. Sometimes even a piece of cheese or a sack of wheat was exchanged for a Cane Corso puppy.

Indiveri found that there was considerable variety in the dogs he came across, noticing in particular that Cane Corsi in the interior regions had a little more coat than those on the plains, presumably because of different climate. All had powerful muscles and were both speedy and very agile, being extremely adept at guarding sheep and the like. None had any wrinkles, folds or dewlaps, and the ears were always cut off. The reason for this, said the peasant farmers, was that the Cane could run into stray dogs or wolves (no ears gave the opponent less to hold on to if a fight ensued). The arcane method of cutting the ears was by the use of scissors and the application of ash and olive oil.

Breeders were primarily interested in the work that their dogs could perform. Although most did not breed for strong teeth, some were used for hunting and as holding dogs, so these tended to have short muzzles and powerful mandibles to enable a better hold. The butchers who used their dogs to watch over swine and cattle equally needed these characteristics. This resulted in slightly convergent cranio-facial axes, so Indiveri felt that slightly jutting teeth was a normal, natural characteristic.

Indiveri studied the Cane Corso on his travels for 20 years and never saw breeds such as

PROTECTING AND PROTECTED

When Cane Corso were used to protect cattle, they wore spiked iron collars to help protect them against wolves. This was called a *vraccale*.

Boxers, Rottweilers, Bullmastiffs or Mastiffs chained anywhere in the countryside of Puglia, where people only had about one litter each year to rejuvenate the "dog park." He felt, therefore, that it was unlikely that the blood of other breeds was included in such breeding. However, if any foreign blood were introduced, this would more likely to have been in areas where there were dog fights, because people constantly tried to breed the fiercest competitor.

Indiveri is adamant that the breed has been recovered, not reconstructed, as is sometimes said. In his own breeding, he was most careful of selection, always trying to go back to the genealogy, combing areas house by house. He and other breeders worked in parallel, and always in collaboration with the SACC. However, he is not alone in accepting that, especially when the breed was in its "boom years." Some people cared only about sales, rather than selection, and mixed in blood of other breeds. Since the breed's gaining official recognition, this practice has been somewhat blocked. In consequence, speculators are now disappearing, and more uniformity is evident.

To sum up, Indiveri believes that the only principal differences in the Cane Corso today are by reason of their being better cared for; in earlier days, they were only fed on wet bread, bran and whey. Noticeable differences will be soon in a well-fed dog, but the type is the same. In his personal opinion, the breed standard should certainly not be changed.

THE BREED NAME

The Cane Corso is also known as the Italian Mastiff or as the Sicilianos Branchiero. However, some consider the Branchiero to be slightly different, as it has smooth hair without an undercoat (*pelo raso*), while the Cane Corso has cow hair that is short and with undercoat (*pelo di vacca*).

The mastiff-type dog of yore, depicted in an illustration by the noted canine artist Reinagle. This drawing appeared in *The Sportsmen's Cabinet* in 1803 and was captioned "Clearly a Molossus."

Cane is Latin for "dog," and is pronounced "ca-nay," while *corso* means "course" or "chase." Hence, the name Cane Corso is usually taken to mean "dog of the chase." However, others theorize that the breed's name derives from the Greek word *kortos*, which means property enclosed by a fence, and so they consider Cane Corso to mean "dog that guards the property." Another connection is the Latin word *cohors*, meaning "protector" or "bodyguard."

In Italy, local dialects have given rise to the breed's having an even wider range of names, including Can'Curs, Can'Guzzo, Cane-E-Presa and sometimes just Molosso. Other names have referred to the dog's duties, so that a butcher's dog was Cane di Maccelaio and a carter's dog Cane di Carretiere.

THE CANE CORSO IN THE UNITED STATES

The Cane Corso first arrived in the US in the late 1980s, imported by the Sottile family of northern New Jersey. Michael Sottile was then a well-known breeder of Rottweilers and Neapolitan Mastiffs, and, since his involvement with the Cane Corso, the breed has continually gained ground in America. However, these early imports were of unverifiable lineage, for at that time there was no functioning registry in Italy.

Initially the breed was judged on the standard written by Michael Sottile, and it is likely that he based this standard on the dogs he imported himself. There was much debate concerning whether changes needed to be made, and in March 2000 a revised standard was published by the ICCF. The ICCF holds events for the breed, including their national specialty. The Cane Corso also is registered with ARBA (the American Rare Breed Association); this is an organization that registers and sponsors events for rare breeds, most of which are not recognized by the American Kennel Club. The breed standard used by ARBA is that of the ICCF. The Cane Corso Preservation Society (CCPS) in the US has ties with SACC, the Italian parent club, and uses the FCI standard.

In the US, there is still debate about the differences between American Cane Corsi and Italian ones, of which the American dogs are larger with longer muzzles. It is perhaps

COMBAT PRACTICE
An 18th-century painting by Hackart shows the Cane Corso in an amphitheater, preparing for combat against the wild boar.

worthy of note that the Cane Corso appears in a wider range of colors in the US than it does in Italy.

THE CANE CORSO IN EUROPE
The Cane Corso is now known in various European countries outside its homeland, such as Germany and France, where the first Cane Corso litter was bred in 1990, although with the provision that no bitches born could be sold in France. Since then, breed registrations in France have risen enormously.

In Britain, the Cane Corso made its first official appearance at a seminar in 1999 at which the Neapolitan Mastiff and Dogue de Bordeaux were the two breeds featured principally. However, the event gave interested parties an ideal opportunity to see the magnificent Cane Corso, which is new to British shores but has undoubtedly captured many hearts.

In Holland, the CCCN has been operating since 1997 and received official recognition in August of 2000. Other countries where the breed is known include Hungary, the Czech Republic, Russia and Denmark.

Molosser expert Christopher Habig of Germany, speaking at a seminar in Britain regarding the Cane Corso in that country. At the time of the seminar in 1999, 13 of the breed were in the UK, and some of these dogs were present for assessment.

An imposing, powerful mastiff, the Cane Corso makes an effective guard dog by looks alone! The breed must be trained carefully in order to enhance its traits of loyalty and protection, never encouraging aggression.

CANE CORSO

The Cane Corso is a large, powerful, intelligent and attractive dog, and, when properly raised, can make a fine companion. However, this is certainly not a breed for everyone and few would recommend a Cane Corso for first-time dog owners, for experience in handling is a tremendous asset for any Cane owner. The breed needs a good deal of attention and physical exercise, and requires socialization both with people and with other dogs.

PERSONALITY

An even-minded dog, the Cane Corso is a highly capable watchdog and protection dog, and this should always be borne in mind. The breed is sometimes described as an aggressive dog, and although this is true to a certain extent, the dog should only be aggressive when he is aware of danger and should never show aggression without good reason. The Cane can be suspicious of strangers but, if properly brought up and socialized, is usually friendly. In fact, it is often said that this breed is born suspicious and therefore needs to be guided as to what is accepted as good behavior.

With his close family, the Cane Corso is a grand companion, usually getting along well with children and other pets, but he will understandably wish to challenge anyone or anything that he considers a threat to those he loves. Although the Cane is generally gentle with children, he should not be given the job of baby-sitting. Children, especially toddlers, can unwittingly cause a dog pain and might just try his patience. Likewise, because the Cane Corso is so powerful, it is unwise for an owner of any age to engage in rough play, for accidents might just happen, albeit unwittingly.

Owners should never underestimate the power of the breed. If not socialized and trained from an early age, a Cane Corso may well become difficult to control. If a Cane Corso has not been brought up and trained with other dogs, he will almost certainly be dog-aggressive. A Cane will not usually start a fight but, if provoked by a strange dog, he will respond immediately and will not back down from the aggressor. For this reason, it is essential to obedience-train a Cane. Understanding of the "No" and "Stop" commands is essential if dog fights are to be prevented.

Given the breed's historical background, it goes without saying that the Cane Corso loves to work and is usually happy to learn any job his owner cares to teach him. The breed makes a fine hunting, trail or police dog and, because of his intelligence, can often work independently.

PHYSICAL CHARACTERISTICS

The Cane Corso is a distinguished and powerful animal of medium to large size, though of slimmer build than his cousin, the Neapolitan Mastiff. His muscles are long and powerful, and this is a breed that expresses not only strength but also agility and endurance. The Cane is slightly longer in body than he is in height at the withers.

The breed's strong, compact body is very muscular, while the lumbar region has to be short and wide, muscular and solid, and, when seen from the side, slightly convex. The croup is long, wide and quite round, due to muscle.

An interesting proportion in the highly detailed Fédération Cynologique Internationale (FCI) standard, which is the standard of the breed's homeland, is that the height of the limbs at the elbows is equal to 50% of the height at withers, making this a well-proportioned animal that is not extremely "leggy."

The forefeet are round in shape, resembling those of a cat, while the hindfeet are slightly more oval, with less arched toes. Nails are strong, curved and well pigmented. Indeed, the pigment under the feet must also be dark, and mucous membranes are black. The skin of the Cane is rather thick, but should adhere to the layers below, while the neck is almost without dewlap.

HEAD

The Cane Corso is a brachycephalic breed, meaning that it is relatively short in foreface, though it is by no means as short as in many other brachycephalic breeds. In the United States, the breed tends to

---

LEADER OF THE PACK

Socializing the Cane Corso from an early age is of the utmost importance if he is to fit well into his environment. Basic training can begin as early as eight weeks of age, paying special attention to interaction with adults, children and other dogs. It is important that your Cane knows that you are the pack leader.

have a longer muzzle, with a less-marked stop. When measured at the cheekbones, the circumference of the head is more than twice the total length of the head. The muzzle is very broad and deep, its width almost equal to its length. The lips are rather firm and when viewed from the front form an upside-down "U" shape; viewed from the side, they hang moderately. The Cane Corso's head should not have wrinkles.

The Cane Corso has black pigmentation and wide nostrils that are well opened and mobile. Teeth are large and white, with complete dentition. The bite should be slightly undershot.

Eyes are intelligent and alert, and are of medium size in comparison with the size of the dog. The eyes should be as dark as possible in accordance with coat color. The third eyelid is to be strongly pigmented, and eyerims are black.

DOMINANT NATURE

Until recent times, Cane Corsi were bred only for their working abilities; indeed, they did not leave their farms until 1988. It should therefore always be borne in mind that the Cane has a dominant nature, especially toward other dogs. If raised with other animals, he should get along with them well, but remember that he will never back down if challenged.

EARS

Ears are of medium size in relation to the volume of the head, and are covered in short hair. Set high and with a wide base, they are triangular, with a rather pointed apex and thick cartilage. When hanging, they fall to the cheeks, and they become semi-erect when the dog is alert. In countries in which ear-cropping is allowed, they are usually cut in an equilateral-triangular shape.

Going back to his early use as a "catch dog," the Cane has always been known for speed and agility that belie his large size.

TAIL

The tail is set quite high on the line of the rump, is thick at the root and is not too tapered. In countries where docking is permissible, the tail is cut at the fourth joint. When left long, it should not much exceed the hock joint when stretched. When the dog is not in action, the tail is held low. At other times, the tail is held horizontal or slightly higher than the back, but it must never be in a vertical position nor should it form a ring.

As with all mastiff breeds, the Cane Corso's impressive head is an important feature. This cropped-eared dog shows the desirable alert expression and required black pigmentation.

Size requirements vary from country to country, but it is universally accepted that the Cane is a large dog that must retain mobility and capability of high speed. This dog carries the characteristic thick tail, docked to the usual length.

SIZE

Males range between 64–68 cm (25.25–26.75 in) and bitches are a little smaller, from 60–64 cm (23.5–25.25 in). In both sexes, there is an allowance of 2 cm in either direction. The weight of males is 45–50 kg (99–110 lbs) and bitches are 40–45 kg (88–99 lbs). Weight should be in proportion to height, as specified by ratios in the FCI breed standard.

In the various American standards, there is either no maximum weight limit or a weight limit of 140 lbs (63.6 kg), this leading to some American dogs' being considerably larger than those found in Europe. The ICCF standard states that a minimum height for dogs is 24 in and for bitches is 22 in, while the minimum weight for dogs is 100 lbs and bitches 80 lbs. No maximums are specified, and the standard does state: "While the larger size is preferred, it should not come at the expense of the dog's working ability or movement."

Many people accept that a Cane Corso of the correct size for this breed should be no larger that that which permits the dog to chase at high speed and to catch wild animals such as boar. However, the dog should also have sufficient bodily power to hold the game.

The black and tan coloration seen on this pup is controversial. Although accepted in the US, the pattern shows the influence of the Rottweiler and Doberman Pinscher breeds.

COAT AND COLOR

The coat of the Cane Corso is short, but is not smooth. It is shiny, close-lying, stiff and very dense. There is a light layer that becomes thicker in winter. The hair on the muzzle is very short, and the coat is slightly longer on the withers, rump, back of thighs and tail, but it has no fringing.

Colors specified in the FCI breed standard are black, plum-gray, slate, light gray, light fawn, deer fawn, dark fawn and "tubby," which means there are well-marked stripes on different shades of fawn or gray. On fawn and tubby dogs, the black or gray mask should not extend beyond the eye line. A small white patch on chest, tips of the feet and nose ridge is accepted, but white patches that are too wide are disqualifying faults. Colors not listed in the FCI standard are also disqualified under FCI rules.

In America, the Cane Corso is found in other colors, including blue and black and tan, and black

A striking black dog with a small white chest patch, acceptable according to the various standards.

with tan and white can also sometimes be seen. The Cane Corso standard approved by the Federation of International Canines (FIC, *not* FCI) reads, "May come in any color except solid white. White is allowed on the chest and neck. A white blaze on the face is allowed as long as it does not extend beyond the ear line. White allowed on feet." Some American dogs also have a lighter eye color than in Italy, with the FIC standard reading, "The color of the eyes in adult dogs ranges from black to hazel and should correspond to the color of

UNDERSTANDING HUMANS

The Cane Corso is a breed that has had contact with man in social situations and, through this, has learned to interpret human gestures and to react only when necessary. This is an attribute that has helped the breed survive through the centuries until the present day.

the dog's coat." Indeed, differences between Italian and American dogs are can be so striking that some enthusiasts have suggested they be classified as different breeds.

HEALTH CONSIDERATIONS

All breeds encounter health problems of one sort and another, but some are more prevalent in certain breeds than in others. To be forewarned is to be forearmed, so the following section of this chapter is not intended to put fear into those who are considering becoming owners of the Cane Corso. Instead, I hope it will help to enlighten, so that any health problems encountered can be dealt with as early as possible and in the most appropriate manner.

HIP DYSPLASIA

Hip dysplasia, known often as HD, is something that seems to affect the Cane Corso and naturally is cause for concern. It is

The Cane Corso depends on strong, powerful, sound hindquarters for typical movement. Breeders guard against hip dysplasia in their lines by having their dogs tested and only breeding dysplasia-free animals.

GROWING UP HEALTHY
A breed such as the Cane Corso needs good nutrition and plenty of exercise. Calcium supplements are often given, especially during the growth period. A good source of calcium is cottage cheese, which a dog is able to assimilate well and is something a Cane usually loves.

a problem involving the malformation of the ball-and-socket joint at the hip, a developmental condition caused by the interaction of many genes. This results in looseness of the hip joints and, although not always painful, it can cause lameness. Typical movement can be impaired because of excessive wear-and-tear on the joints.

Although a dog's environment does not actually cause hip dysplasia, it may have some bearing on how unstable the hip joint eventually becomes. Osteoarthritis eventually develops as a result of the instability.

Testing schemes for hip dysplasia are available through the Orthopedic Foundation for Animals. Both hips are tested and scored individually; the lower the score, the less the degree of dysplasia. Clearly, dogs with scores higher than the specified norm should not be incorporated in breeding programs.

DO YOU KNOW ABOUT HIP DYSPLASIA?

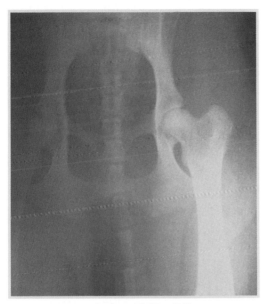

X-ray of a dog with "Good" hips.

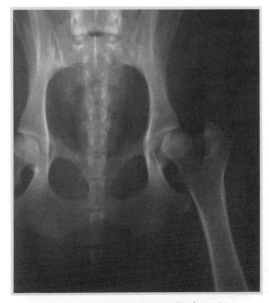

X-ray of a dog with "Moderate" dysplastic hips.

Hip dysplasia is a fairly common condition found in pure-bred dogs. When a dog has hip dysplasia, his hind leg has an incorrectly formed hip joint. By constant use of the hip joint, it becomes more and more loose, wears abnormally and may become arthritic.

Hip dysplasia can only be confirmed with an x-ray, but certain symptoms may indicate a problem. Your dog may have a hip dysplasia problem if he walks in a peculiar manner, hops instead of smoothly runs, uses his hind legs in unison (to keep the pressure off the weak joint), has trouble getting up from a prone position or always sits with both legs together on one side of his body.

As the dog matures, he may adapt well to life with a bad hip, but in a few years the arthritis develops and many dogs with hip dysplasia become crippled. Hip dysplasia is considered an inherited disease and only can be diagnosed definitively by x-ray when the dog is two years old, although symptoms often appear earlier. Some experts claim that a special diet might help your puppy outgrow the bad hip, but the usual treatments are surgical. The removal of the pectineus muscle, the removal of the round part of the femur, reconstructing the pelvis and replacing the hip with an artificial one are all surgical interventions that are expensive, but they are usually very successful. Follow the advice of your veterinarian.

GASTRIC TORSION (BLOAT)

Gastric torsion, also known as bloat, is a rapid accumulation of gas and liquid in the stomach of a dog. This accumulation distends the stomach, leading to blockage of the sphincter. The stomach can also become displaced, twisting around on itself, again blocking the sphincter. This can lead rapidly to death, so veterinary attention must be sought as a matter of urgency as soon as symptoms are noticed. Surgery can be successful but, regrettably, the post-operative death rate is quite high.

The initial sign is a distended abdomen with copious salivation and unproductive attempts to vomit. Respiratory difficulties ensue, followed by a state of shock. If tapping the abdominal wall creates a drum-like sound, this is indicative of torsion.

Large, deep-chested dogs that gobble their food quickly, gulp air and drink a large amount of liquid immediately after eating are more prone to bloat than others. Sensible preventative advice includes feeding two smaller meals daily instead of one large one, discouraging rapid eating and drinking and offering the dog's food and water in elevated bowl stands, which can be purchased at a pet shop. It is very important not to feed a dog immediately before or after exercise, ideally allowing two hours in between.

CRUCIATE LIGAMENT RUPTURE

The cruciate ligaments that cross each other in the stifle joint are important to maintain stability. Rupture of the cranial cruciate ligament is an injury that can particularly affect larger breeds of dog, more especially those that are old or overweight.

Slight lameness can be improved with rest, but in many cases surgery is necessary. Sometimes the first sign of rupture is sudden, with the dog being in evident pain, but in other cases lameness is intermittent, though gradually worsening with time. Many different surgical techniques are employed to stabilize the stifle, but all require careful post-operative nursing.

SKIN PROBLEMS

Dogs can suffer from a variety of skin problems, and Cane Corsi are no exception. Skin conditions are often difficult to treat successfully, but dietary control and antibacterial shampoo can be helpful. Some skin problems arise as a result of allergy to something as simple as the living room carpet! The earlier the symptoms are found, the sooner they can be dealt with, making life much more comfortable for the dog.

Demodectic mange, also known as red mange, is seen in both dogs and cats and is usually due to an immune defect that fails to keep in check the number of mites, which, interestingly enough, are present on the skin of all animals, including humans. A population explosion results in bacterial infection, and the mites produce substances that compromise the immune system, hence perpetuating the infestation. This type of mange can also be induced by stress, such as when a dog has been shipped abroad or is undergoing hormonal changes. A typical symptom is balding patches, in which the skin is red and itchy. A veterinary skin scrape can diagnose the problem, which is treatable.

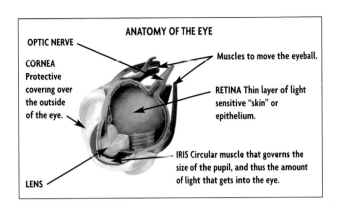

ANATOMY OF THE EYE

OPTIC NERVE

CORNEA Protective covering over the outside of the eye.

LENS

Muscles to move the eyeball.

RETINA Thin layer of light sensitive "skin" or epithelium.

IRIS Circular muscle that governs the size of the pupil, and thus the amount of light that gets into the eye.

EYE PROBLEMS

The eye problems encountered by Cane Corsi are in keeping with those found in other molosser breeds. Entropion is when one or more eyelids curl inwards, causing the lashes to scratch the cornea. This causes irritation, which leads to scarring and eventual ulceration. It can usually be corrected with surgery. Entropion is hereditary and thus is a factor that must be considered carefully when planning a breeding program.

Ectropion is the opposite of entropion; with ectropion, the eyelids roll outward. This affects the lower lids, exposing sensitive tissues that are usually protected. Dogs can be born with this condition, especially if they are heavily wrinkled, or it can occur as a result of injury or scarring. Ectropion can also cause the third eyelid to become inflamed and infected. Sometimes the same dog can suffer from both entropion and ectropion; in this case, the upper lids roll inwards and the lower ones outwards.

"Cherry eye" (glandular hypertrophy) is often found in Cane Corsi. This is sometimes prompted by ectropion, but not always. This is actually an enlargement of the nictitating membrane in the inner corner of the eye, so that it looks like a small red cherry. This usually appears in puppies, and can be remedied either by surgical removal or, as is more frequently done, by tacking it back into place. However, the latter is not always successful, in which case removal will be necessary. Occasionally the swelling will disappear, but it often reappears again relatively soon afterwards.

BREED STANDARD FOR THE

CANE CORSO

INTRODUCTION TO THE BREED STANDARD

There are various breed standards currently in use for the Cane Corso, but the most widely recognized is the FCI standard, of which a translation is presented here. It gives very specific measurements and proportions, detailing the ideal characteristics of the breed as well as different degrees of faults. This translation employs specific anatomical terminology that may be unfamiliar to many readers.

All breed standards are designed effectively to paint a picture in words, though each reader will almost certainly have a slightly different way of interpreting these words. After all, were everyone to interpret a breed standard in exactly the same way, there would only be one consistent winner within the breed at any given time! In any event, to fully comprehend the intricacies of a breed, reading words alone is never enough. In addition, it is essential for devotees to give themselves every opportunity to come into contact with as many

Cane Corsi as possible. In countries where the breed is actively shown, it is important to watch them being judged in the ring. This enables owners to absorb as much as possible about the breed they love. "Hands-on" experience, providing an opportunity to assess the structure of dogs, is always valuable, especially for those who hope ultimately to judge the breed.

A breed standard undoubtedly helps breeders to perpetuate desirable breed type by producing stock that comes as close as possible to the recognized standard. It also helps the show judge to know exactly what he is looking for in the conformation ring. This enables the judge to make a carefully considered decision when selecting the most typical Cane Corso present to head the line of winners.

However familiar you are with the breed, it is always worth refreshing your memory by re-reading the standard. It is sometimes all too easy to overlook, or perhaps conveniently forget, certain features.

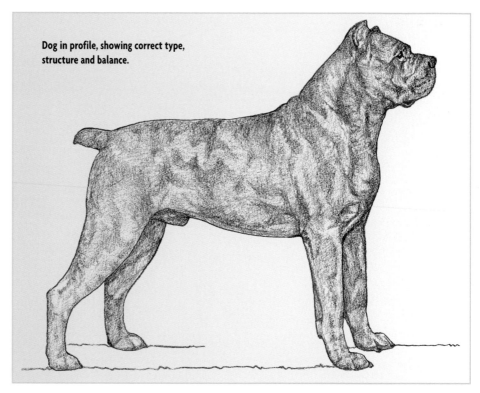

Dog in profile, showing correct type, structure and balance.

THE FCI STANDARD FOR THE CANE CORSO (FCI STANDARD #343)

ORIGIN
Italy.

UTILIZATION
Watch, protection, police and track dog.

FCI CLASSIFICATION
Group 2 Dogs: Pinschers and Schnauzers, Molossians and Swiss Mountain and Cattle Dogs; Section 2: Molossians, with Working Trial.

BRIEF HISTORICAL SUMMARY
Its direct ancestor is the *Canis Pugnax* (the old Roman Molossian) of which he is the light version employed in the hunting of large wild animals and also as an "auxiliary warrior" in battles. For years he has been a precious companion of the Italian populations. Employed as property, cattle and personal guard dog and used for hunting purposes, too. In the past this breed was common all over Italy as an ample iconography and historiography testify. In the recent past he has found a

excellent preservation area in southern Italy, especially in Puglia, Lucania and Sannio. His name derives from the Latin *Cohors* which means "guardian," "protector."

GENERAL APPEARANCE

Medium-big size dog, strongly built but elegant, with powerful and long muscles, very distinguished, he expresses strength, agility and endurance. The general conformation is that of a mesomorphic animal whose body is longer than the height at the withers, harmonious as regards the form and disharmonious as regards the profile.

IMPORTANT PROPORTIONS

The length of the body is about 11% over the height at the withers. The total length of the head reaches 3.6/10 of the height at the withers. The length of the muzzle is equal to 3.4/10 of the total length of the head. The height of the thorax is 5/10 of the height at the withers and it is equal to the height of the limb at the elbows.

BEHAVIOR AND TEMPERAMENT

Intelligent, active and even-minded, he is an unequaled watchdog and protection dog. Docile and affectionate with the owner, loving with children and with the family, if necessary he becomes a brave protector of people, house and property. He is easily trained.

HEAD

Brachycephalic. Its total length reaches 3.6/10 of the height at the withers. The bizygomatic width, which is equal to the length of the skull, is more than half the total height of the head, reaching 6.6/10. The upper longitudinal axes of the skull and of the muzzle are slightly convergent The perimeter of the head, measured at the cheekbones, is more than twice the total length of the head, even in the females. The head is moderately sculptured with zygomatic arches stretched outwards. The skin is firm and sticking to the tissues underneath; it is smooth and quite stretched. **Cranial Region:** *Skull*—Seen from the front, it is wide and slightly curved, seen from the side it draws an irregular curve that, accentuated in the subregion of the forehead, becomes flat along

---

AKC FSS

In America, the Cane Corso is accepted for recording on the American Kennel Club's Foundation Stock Service. This is a service provided to allow new breeds to develop with the security of a reliable way of maintaining records. The Cane Corso is not yet eligible for AKC recognition.

the external saggital crest. Seen from the top, it looks square because of the outstretching of the zygomatic arches and the powerful muscles swathing it. Frontal sinuses well developed and stretched forward, deep forehead hollow and visible median furrow. Occipital crest not much developed. Supraorbital fossae slightly marked.

Stop—Very marked because of the very developed and bulging frontal sinuses and because of the prominent superciliary arches. **Facial Region:** *Nose*—It is on the same line as the nose pipe. Seen from the side, it mustn't stick out from the front vertical margin of the lips but be, with its front, on the same vertical line as the front of the muzzle. It has to be voluminous, rather flat on top, with wide nostrils, opened and mobile, wet and cool. The pigmentation is black.

Muzzle—Very broad and deep. The width of the muzzle must be almost equal to its length, which reaches 3.4/10 of the total length of the head. Its depth is more than 50% the length of the muzzle. Due to the parallels of the muzzle sides and to the fullness and the width of the whole jaw, the anterior face of the muzzle is flat and square. The nasal bridge has a rectilinear profile and it is rather flat. The lower side profile of the muzzle is determined by the upper lips; the suborbital region shows a very slight chisel.

Lips—Rather firm. Seen from the front, the upper lips form at their disjunction an upside down "U" and, seen from the side, hang moderately. The commisure is rightly evident and it always represents the lowest point of the lower side profile of the muzzle. The pigmentation is black.

Jaws—Very wide, strong and thick, with a very slight shortening of the upper jaw with a subsequent light prognathism (undershot mouth). The branches of the lower jaw are very strong and, seen from the side, are quite curved, the body of the lower jaw, well accentuated forward, points out well the marked chin. The incisors are firmly placed on a straight line.

Cheeks—The masseter region is full and evident, but not hypertrophic.

Teeth—White, big, complete in growth and number. The lower jaw incisors pass only slightly (about 1/2 cm) their correspon-

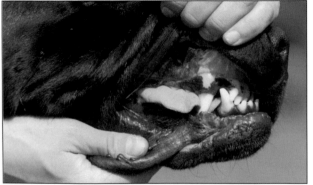

A Cane Corso's teeth should be large and the bite should be slightly undershot.

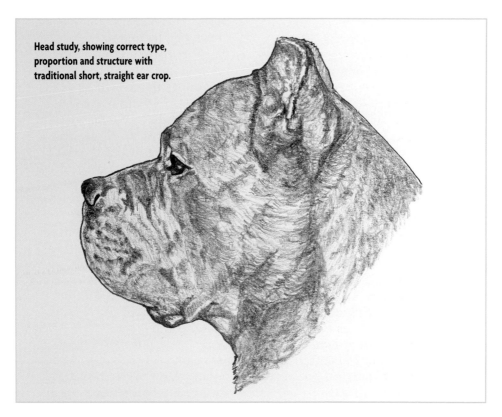

Head study, showing correct type, proportion and structure with traditional short, straight ear crop.

dent ones on the upper arch, so the bite is slightly undershot.

Eyes—Of medium size compared to the size of the dog, in a sub-frontal position, well spaced. *Rima palpebrarum* nearly oval, eyeballs slightly protruding, eyelids with the borders pigmented with black. The eye mustn't let the sclera be seen. Third eyelid strongly pigmented. Iris as dark as possible according to the color of the coat. Look intelligent and alert.

Ears—Of medium size in relation to the volume of the head and to the size of the dog; covered with short hair, of triangular shape.

NECK
Topline: Slightly arched.
Length: 3.6/10 of the height at the withers, that is equal to the total length of the head.
Shape: Of oval section, strong, very muscular, with a marked disjunction form at the nape. The perimeter, at half length of the neck, is about 8/10 of the height at the withers. Harmoniously joined with the withers, shoulder and chest, the neck has its ideal

direction at 45° from the ground and at right angle with the shoulder.

Skin: The lower margin of the neck is practically without dewlap.

BODY

Compact, strong and very muscular. Its length is 11% over the height at the withers, with allowance of ±1%.

Topline: The back region is rectilinear with a slightly lumbar convexity.

Withers: They clearly rise on the dorsal line and over the rump level, are high, long, wide. They are lean and join harmoniously to the neck and to the back.

Back: It is wide, very muscular as the whole upper line of the trunk, slightly climbing from the back to the front and with a strictly rectilinear profile. Its length is approx. 32% of the height at the withers.

Loins: The lumbar region has to be short, wide, well joined to the back and to the rump, very muscular, very solid and, seen from the side, slightly convex. Its length, slightly higher than its width, is equal to 20% of the height at the withers.

Croup: It is long, wide, quite round due to the considerable growth of the muscles. The length, measured from the ridge of the hip to the ridge of the nates is equal to 32% of the height at the

withers. Its average width is equal to 23% of the height at the withers, its inclination on the horizontal line, on the basis of the ilium-ischiatic line is of 28°/30°, on the basis of the line from the ridge of the hip to the insertion of the tail is of 15°/16°. Therefore, the rump is slightly inclined.

Chest: Wide, well inclined and open, with well-developed muscles. Its width, in close relation with the width of the thorax, reaches 35% of the height to the withers; the breastbone is at the same height as the tip of the shoulders. Seen from the side, the chest is outstretched forward between the forelegs and slightly convex.

Thorax: It has to be well developed in the three dimensions with long, oblique, wide and well shaped ribs with wide intercostal spaces. The four false ribs are long, oblique and open. The thorax reaches down at the elbow and its height is equal to half the height at the withers. Its width, measured at half of its height, is equal to 35% of the height at the withers and decreases slightly towards the sternum region without forming a carina. The depth (saggital diameter) is equal to 55% the height at the withers. Its perimeter is over 35% the height at the withers.

Underline and belly: The sternum region is lean, long, wide and seen from the side it outlines a

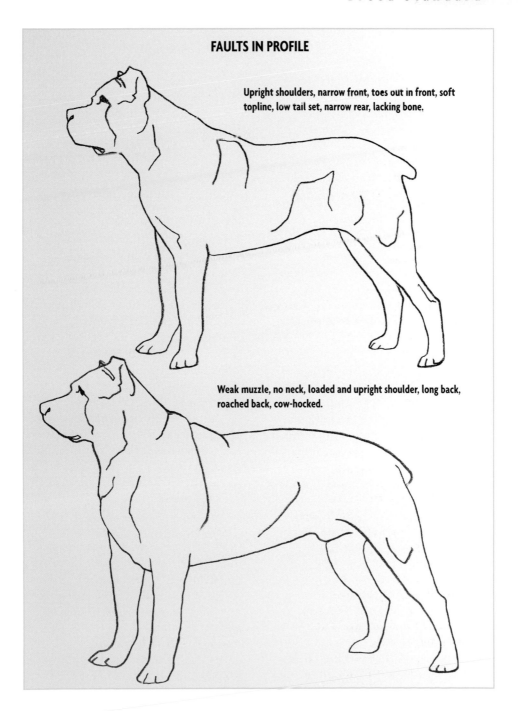

FAULTS IN PROFILE

Upright shoulders, narrow front, toes out in front, soft toplinc, low tail set, narrow rear, lacking bone.

Weak muzzle, no neck, loaded and upright shoulder, long back, roached back, cow-hocked.

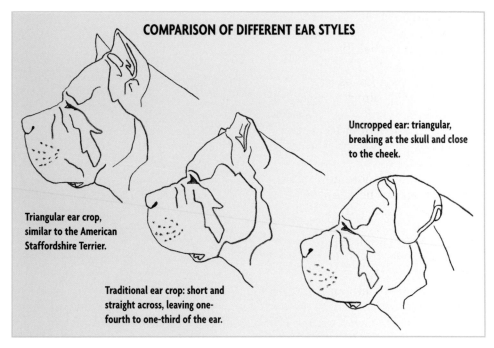

COMPARISON OF DIFFERENT EAR STYLES

Uncropped ear: triangular, breaking at the skull and close to the cheek.

Triangular ear crop, similar to the American Staffordshire Terrier.

Traditional ear crop: short and straight across, leaving one-fourth to one-third of the ear.

semicircle with a wide radius which caudally goes up smoothly to the abdomen. The abdomen region is neither hollowed nor relaxed and, seen from the side, rises up from the sternum edge to the groins with a smooth curve. The hollow on the side is not very marked.

Tail: It is inserted quite high on the rump line, thick at the root and not too tapering at the tip, and if stretched is not too much over the hock. When not in action, is low. Otherwise is horizontal or slightly higher than the back, it must never be bent to form a ring or in a vertical position. It gets amputated at the fourth vertebrae.

LIMBS

Forequarters: Perpendicular, seen from the front or in profile. The height of the limbs at the elbows is equal to 50% of the height at the withers. Well proportioned to the size of the dog. Strong and powerful.

Shoulder—Long, oblique, strong, equipped with long, powerful and well divided muscles, is adherent to the thorax but free in movement. Its length, from the top of the withers to the ridge of the shoulder, is equal to 30% of the height at the withers and its inclination on the horizontal line is between 48°/50°. In relation to the median plane of the body, the ridges of the shoulder blades are slightly swerved.

Arm—It is slightly longer than the shoulder, strong, with very well developed bones and muscles, well joined to the trunk in its top 2/3, measured from the ridge of the shoulder to the tip of the elbow, it has a length equal to 31/32% of the height at the withers and an inclination with the horizontal line of approx. 58°/60°. Its longitudinal direction is parallel to the median plane of the body. The angle between the shoulder blades and the humerus is between 106° and 110°.

Elbows—The elbows, long and protruding, adherent but not too close to the rib cage, covered with lean skin, must be like the humeri, on a strictly parallel plane to the sagittal plane of the trunk. The tip of the elbow (olecranon epiphysis) is located on the vertical line lowered from the caudal (or back) angle of the shoulder blade to the ground.

Forearm—It is perfectly vertical, oval section, with several muscles, in particular in the top-third, with a very strong and compact bone structure. Its length, from the tip of the elbow to the tip of the arm is equal to 32/33% of the height at the withers. Its perimeter, measured straight underneath the elbow, is equal to 39% of the height at the withers, the carpus-cubital groove is quite marked.

Carpal joint—Seen from the front, it follows the straight vertical line of the forearm; it is lean, wide, mobile, thick. Its perimeter reaches 26% of height at the withers, at its top margin the pisiform bone is strongly projected backwards.

Pastern—It is quite smaller than the forearm, is very strong, lean, elastic, slightly flexed (it forms with the ground an angle of approx. 75°). Its length must not be over one-sixth of the height of the forelimb at the elbow. Seen from the front, it follows the perpendicular line of the forearm and of the carpus.

Forefeet—They have a round shape, with very arched, tight toes (cat's foot). Lean and hard soles. The nails are strong, curved and pigmented, there is a good pigmentation also in the plantar and digital pads.

Hindquarters: Perpendicular, seen from the front or in profile. Well proportioned to the size of the dog, strong and powerful.

Thigh—It is long and wide, with prominent muscles, therefore the nate ridge is well marked. Its length is over 33% of the height at the withers and the width is never lower than 25% of such height. The thigh-bone axis, quite oblique from the top to the bottom and from the back to the front, has an inclination of 70° on the horizontal line and forms with the coxal axis an angle which is

The protruding hock ridge shows clearly the continuation of the leg groove. The distance from the ridge of the hock to the sole of the foot (to the ground) shouldn't be over 26% of the height at the withers. Its direction, in relation to the median plane of the body is parallel. The tibio-metatarsal angle is of approx 140°.

Hock (Metatarsus)—It is very thick, lean, rather short, cylindrical, and always perpendicular to the ground. Seen from the side and from the back, its length is equal to approx 15% of the height at the withers (tarsus and foot excluded). Its internal side has to present itself without spur.

Hindfeet—They have a slightly more oval shape than the fore ones and a less arched toes.

slightly more than right (coxo-femural angle).

Second thigh—It is long, lean, with a strong bone and muscle structure, has a well-marked muscular groove. Its length is equal to 32% of the height at the withers and its inclination from the top to the bottom and from the front to the back is of approx. 50° on the horizontal line.

Stifle—The angle of the stifle joint, is of approx. 120°. Its direction is parallel to the median plane of the body.

Hock joint—It is wide, thick, clean, with well-marked bone.

GAIT/MOVEMENT
Long steps, stretched trot, some steps of gallop, but with inclination to stretched trot.

SKIN
It is, rather thick, has limited subcutaneous connective tissue and therefore is adherent everywhere to the layers underneath. The neck is practically without dewlap. The head mustn't have wrinkles. The pigment of the mucous membranes is black. The pigment of the soles and the nails must be dark.

COAT

Hair: Short hair but not smooth, with vitreous texture, shiny, adherent, stiff, very dense, with a light layer that becomes thicker in winter (but never crops up on the covering hair). Its average length is approx. 2/2.5 cm. On the withers, the rump, the back margin of the thighs and on the tail it reaches approx. 3 cm without creating fringes. On the muzzle the hair is very short, smooth, adherent and is not more than 1/1.5 cm.

Color: Black, plum-gray, slate, light gray, light fawn, deer fawn, dark fawn and tubby (very well marked stripes on different shades of fawn and gray). In the fawny and tubby subjects, there is a black or gray mask only on the muzzle and shouldn't go beyond the eye line. A small white patch on the chest, on the feet tips or on the nose bridge is accepted.

HEIGHT AND WEIGHT

Height at the withers: For males from 64 cm to 68 cm. For females from 60 cm to 64 cm. With allowance of ± 2 cm.

Weight: Males from 45 to 50 kg. Ratio weight/size 0.710 (kg/cm). Females from 40 to 45 kg. Ratio weight/size 0.680 (kg/cm).

FAULTS

Any departure from the foregoing points should be considered a fault and the seriousness with which the fault should be regarded should be in exact proportion to its degree and diffusion.

Severe Faults: *Head*—Accentuated parallelism of the axes of the skull and the muzzle. Very marked converging axes of the skull and the muzzle. Converging side lines of the muzzle. Scissors bite. Pronounced and disturbing undershot mouth.

Nose—Partial depigmentation.

Tail—Forming a ring or in a vertical position.

Size—Oversize or undersize.

Gait/movement—Continued amble.

Disqualifying Faults: *Head*—Diverging axes of the skull and the muzzle. Overshot mouth. Nose bridge resolutely hollow or ram-like.

Nose—Total depigmentation.

Eyes—Partial and bilateral palpebral depigmentation. Wall-eye. Bilateral strabismus.

Sexual organs—Monorchidism. Cryptorchidism. Obvious incomplete growth of one or both testicles.

Tail—Tailless, short-tail, artificial or congenital.

Hair—Semi-long, smooth, fringed.

Colors—All colors not prescribed, white patches too wide.

NOTE

Males should have two apparently normal testicles fully descended into the scrotum.

CANE CORSO

SELECTING A BREEDER AND PUPPY

Before reaching the decision that you will definitely look for a Cane Corso puppy, it is essential that you are clear that this is absolutely the most suitable breed for you and for your family. You should have carefully weighed your family situation and living environment, and it is important for you to realize just how powerful an adult Cane Corso will become. Not only will a breed of this size take up a fair amount of space around the home, it will also cost considerably more to feed than would a small breed. You must also be sure that you want a Cane Corso for the right reasons, and that you are prepared to establish your own authority over the dog in order to bring up a well-adjusted, sensibly behaved companion.

Before beginning your search, you should do plenty of "homework" on the breed, which includes seeing as many Cane Corsi as possible with their breeders and owners. Dog shows are wonderful opportunities to do this. When selecting a breeder, you will have to consider advice and form your own opinions

"YOU BETTER SHOP AROUND!"

Finding a reputable breeder who sells healthy pups is very important, but make sure that the breeder you choose is not only someone you respect but also someone with whom you feel comfortable. Your breeder will be a resource long after you buy your puppy, and you must be able to call with reasonable questions without being made to feel like a pest! If you don't connect on a personal level, investigate some other breeders before making a final decision.

about which breeders are the most dedicated ones. A careful breeder will have put much thought into planning a litter, will have considered health issues and will have given all puppies in the litter tho very best start in life.

Once you are absolutely certain that the Cane Corso is the breed for you, and you have selected a responsible breeder, you must discuss your family situation and your intentions for your dog with the breeder, taking his advice as to which puppy is likely to suit you best. Remember that the dog you select should remain with you for the duration of his life, which is usually from 10 to 12 years, so making the right decision from the outset is of utmost importance. No dog should be moved from one home to another simply because the owners were thoughtless enough not to have done sufficient research on the breed, the breeder and the background of the litter before selecting the puppy. It is always important to remember that, when looking for a puppy, a good breeder will be assessing

you as a prospective new owner just as carefully as you are selecting the breeder.

Cane Corso breed clubs like the ICCF and CCPS and national canine organizations such as ARBA can point you in the direction of ethical, reputable breeders. The breed is relatively rare in the US, but you should be able to find a good breeder in your state or region. Once you have contacted and met a breeder or two and made your choice about which breeder is best suited to your needs, it's time to visit the litter.

Keep in mind that many top breeders have waiting lists, especially with a rare breed like the Cane Corso. Sometimes new owners have to wait a year or more for a puppy. If you are really committed to the breeder whom

Take the opportunity to meet all dogs on the breeder's premises, puppies and adults alike. This will give you a good idea of how the breeder's line matures in type, soundness and temperament.

ARE YOU A FIT OWNER?
If the breeder from whom you are buying a puppy asks you a lot of personal questions, do not be insulted. Such a breeder wants to be sure that you will be a fit provider for his puppy.

you've selected, then you will wait (and hope for an early arrival!). If not, you may have to choose another breeder with whom you feel comfortable. Don't be too anxious, however. If the breeder doesn't have a waiting list, or any customers, there is probably a good reason. It's no different than visiting a restaurant with no clientele. The better establishments always have waiting lists—and it's usually worth the wait. Besides, isn't a puppy more important than a nice dinner?

Breeders commonly allow visitors to see their litters by around the fifth or sixth week, and puppies leave for their new homes between the eighth and tenth week. Breeders who permit their puppies to leave early are more interested in making a profit than in their puppies' well-being. Puppies need to learn the rules of

INHERIT THE MIND
In order to know whether or not a puppy will fit into your lifestyle, you need to assess his personality. A good way to do this is to interact with his parents. Your pup inherits not only his appearance but also his personality and temperament from the sire and dam. If the parents are fearful or overly aggressive, these same traits may likely show up in your puppy.

the pack from their dam, and most dams continue teaching the pups manners and dos and don'ts until around the eighth week. Breeders spend significant amounts of time with the Cane Corso toddlers so that the pups are able to interact with the "other species," i.e., humans. Given the long history that dogs and humans have, bonding between the two species is natural but must be nurtured. A well-bred, well-socialized Cane pup wants nothing more than to be near you and please you.

When visiting a litter, all puppies should have been well socialized and should look well fed, but not pot-bellied, as this might indicate worms. Eyes should look bright and clear, without discharge. Their noses should be moist, an indication of good health, but never runny. It goes without saying that there should be no evidence of loose stools or parasites. The pups should have

If you can provide the right living environment, leadership and care for the Cane Corso, your choice of this breed will be a very rewarding one for all members of the family.

short coats that look healthy, an important indicator of good health internally. Also remember that a slightly undershot bite is correct in this breed.

Something else you should consider before making your selection is whether you have a preference for a male or female. There are a few differences to think about. Males are generally larger than bitches, and they are also more dominant and more likely to challenge their owners for leadership of the pack. Upon reaching maturity, both sexes are likely to become intolerant of other dogs, but males are especially prone to this.

You may also want to consider a veterinary insurance policy for your puppy. Vet's bills can mount up, and you must always be certain that sufficient funds are available to give your dog any veterinary attention that may be needed. As this type of insurance is becoming more and more popular, there is a wide range of coverage available. Discuss this with your vet.

COMMITMENT OF OWNERSHIP
After considering all of the factors associated with owning a dog, you have most likely already made some very important decisions about selecting your puppy. You have chosen the Cane Corso, which means that you have decided which characteristics you

PUPPY APPEARANCE
Your puppy should have a well-fed appearance but not a distended abdomen, which may indicate worms or incorrect feeding, or both. The body should be firm, with a solid feel. The skin of the abdomen should be pale pink and clean, without signs of scratching or rash. Check the hind legs to see if the dewclaws were removed, as this is done at only a few days old.

want in a dog and what type of dog will best fit into your family and lifestyle. If you have selected a breeder, you have gone a step further—you have done your research and found a responsible, conscientious person who breeds quality Cane Corsi and who should be a reliable source of help as you and your puppy adjust to life together. If you have observed a litter in action, you have obtained a firsthand look at the dynamics of a puppy "pack" and, thus, you have learned about each pup's individual personality—perhaps you have even found one that particularly appeals to you.

However, even if you have not yet found the Cane puppy of your dreams, observing pups will help you learn to recognize certain behavior and to determine what a pup's behavior indicates about his temperament. You will be able to pick out which pups are the leaders, which ones are less outgoing, which ones are

How will you choose? In addition to taking the breeder's advice, bring the whole family along to meet the litter and see which puppy chooses you!

> ## PUPPY PERSONALITY
>
> When a litter becomes available to you, choosing a pup out of all those adorable faces will not be an easy task! Sound temperament is of utmost importance, but each pup has its own personality and some may be better suited to you than others. A feisty, independent pup will do well in a home with older children and adults, while quiet, shy puppies will thrive in homes with minimal noise and distractions. Your breeder knows the pups best and should be able to guide you in the right direction.

confident, shy, playful, friendly, aggressive, etc. Equally as important, you will learn to recognize what a healthy pup should look and act like. All of these things will help you in your search, and when you find the Cane Corso that was meant for you, you will know it!

Researching your breed, selecting a responsible breeder and observing as many pups as possible are all important steps on the way to dog ownership. It may seem like a lot of effort...and you have not even taken the pup home yet! Remember, though, you cannot be too careful when it comes to deciding on the type of dog you want and finding out about your prospective pup's background. Buying a puppy is not—or *should* not be—just

another whimsical purchase. This is one instance in which you actually do get to choose your own family! You may be thinking that buying a puppy should be fun—it should not be so serious and so much work. Keep in mind that your puppy is not a cuddly stuffed toy or decorative lawn ornament; rather, he is a living creature that will become a real member of your family. You will come to realize that, while buying a puppy is a pleasurable and exciting endeavor, it is not something to be taken lightly. Relax…the fun will start when the pup comes home!

Always keep in mind that a puppy is nothing more than a baby in a furry disguise…a baby who is virtually helpless in a human world and who trusts his owner for fulfillment of his basic needs for survival. In addition to food, water and shelter, your pup needs care, protection, guidance and love. If you are not prepared to commit to this, then you are not prepared to own a dog.

"Wait a minute," you say. "How hard could this be? All of my neighbors own dogs and they seem to be doing just fine. Why should I have to worry about all of this?" Well, you should not worry about it; in fact, you will probably find that once your Cane Corso pup gets used to his new home, he will fall into his place in the family quite naturally.

FEEDING TIPS
You will probably start feeding your pup the same food that he has been getting from the breeder; the breeder should give you a few days' supply to start you off. Although you should not give your pup too many treats, you will want to have puppy treats on hand for coaxing, training, rewards, etc. Be careful, though, as a small pup's calorie requirements are relatively low and a few treats can add up to almost a full day's worth of calories without the required nutrition.

However, it never hurts to emphasize the commitment of dog ownership. With some time and patience, a responsible experienced owner can raise a Cane pup to be a well-adjusted and well-mannered adult dog—a dog that could be your most loyal friend.

PREPARING PUPPY'S PLACE IN YOUR HOME

Researching your breed and finding a breeder are only two aspects of the "homework" you will have to do before taking your Cane puppy home. You will also have to prepare your home and family for the new addition. Much as you would prepare a nursery for a newborn baby, you will need to designate a place in your home that will be the puppy's own. How you prepare your home will depend on how much freedom the dog will be allowed. Whatever you decide, you must ensure that he has a place that he can call his own.

When you take your new puppy into your home, you are bringing him into what will become his home as well. Obviously, you did not buy a puppy with the intentions of catering to his every whim and allowing him to "rule the roost," but in order for a puppy to grow into a stable, well-adjusted dog, he has to feel comfortable in his surroundings. Remember, he is leaving the warmth and security of his mother and littermates, as well as the familiarity of the only place he has ever known, so it is important to make his transition as easy as possible. By preparing a place in your home for the puppy, you are making him feel as welcome as possible in a strange new place. It should

ARE YOU PREPARED?
Unfortunately, when a puppy is bought by someone who does not take into consideration the time and attention that dog ownership requires, it is the puppy who suffers when he is either abandoned or placed in a shelter by a frustrated owner. So all of the "homework" you do in preparation for your pup's arrival will benefit you both. The more informed you are, the more you will know what to expect and the better equipped you will be to handle the ups and downs of raising a puppy. Hopefully, everyone in the household is willing to do his part in raising and caring for the pup. The anticipation of owning a dog often brings a lot of promises from excited family members: "I will walk him every day," "I will feed him," "I will house-train him," etc., but these things take time and effort, and promises can easily be forgotten once the novelty of the new pet has worn off.

not take him long to get used to it, but the sudden shock of being transplanted is somewhat traumatic for a young pup. Imagine how a small child would feel in the same situation—that is how your puppy must be feeling. It is up to you to reassure him and to let him know, "Little *cane*, you are going to like it here!"

The first importer of Cane Corso into Britain, shown with a female and male pair.

WHAT YOU SHOULD BUY

CRATE

To someone unfamiliar with the use of crates in dog training, it may seem like punishment to shut a dog in a crate, but this is not the case at all. Although all breeders do not advocate crate training, more and more breeders and trainers are recommending crates as preferred tools for pet puppies as well as show puppies.

Crates are not cruel—crates have many humane and highly effective uses in dog care and training. For example, crate training is a popular and very successful house-training method. In addition, a crate can keep your dog safe during travel and, perhaps most importantly, a crate provides your dog with a place of his own in your home. It serves as a "doggie bedroom" of sorts—your Cane Corso can curl up in his crate when he wants to sleep or when he just needs a break. Many dogs sleep in their crates overnight, and this is the only time when your pup should be confined for more than an hour or two. With soft bedding and his favorite toy, a crate becomes a

---

YOUR SCHEDULE . . .

If you lead an erratic, unpredictable life, with daily or weekly changes in your work requirements, consider the problems of owning a puppy. The new puppy has to be fed regularly, socialized (loved, petted, handled, introduced to other people) and, most importantly, allowed to go outdoors for house-training. As the dog gets older, he can be more tolerant of deviations in his feeding and relief schedule.

PHOTO COURTESY OF DOSKOCIL

When choosing a crate for your Cane, keep in mind the puppy's rapid growth; it is best to obtain one from the outset that will house your Cane at his full size.

open, allowing the air to flow through and affording the dog a view of what is going on around him, while a fiberglass crate is sturdier. Both can double as travel crates, providing protection for the dog in the car.

The size of the crate is another thing to consider. Puppies do not stay puppies forever—in fact, sometimes it seems as if they grow right before your eyes. A small crate may be fine for a very

cozy pseudo-den for your dog. Large-breed dogs like the Cane should never be confined for long periods, which could negatively effect their physical growth.

As far as purchasing a crate, the type that you buy is up to you. It will most likely be one of the two most popular types: wire or fiberglass. There are advantages and disadvantages to each type. For example, a wire crate is more

PEDIGREE VS. REGISTRATION CERTIFICATE

Too often new owners are confused between these two important documents. Your puppy's pedigree, essentially a family tree, is a written record of a dog's genealogy of three generations or more. The pedigree will show you the names as well as performance titles of all dogs in your pup's background. Your breeder must provide you with a registration application, with his part properly filled out. You must complete the application and send it to the registering organization with the proper fee. The seller must provide you with complete records to identify the puppy. Important information includes the following: breed; sex, color and markings; date of birth; litter number (when available); names and registration numbers of the parents; breeder's name; and date sold or delivered.

Wire crates have many advantages. In this case, the pups are safely confined while enjoying some fresh air and the goings-on of their surroundings.

young Cane Corso pup, but it will not do him much good for long! Unless you have the money and the inclination to buy a new crate every time your pup has a growth spurt, it is better to get one that will accommodate your dog both as a pup and at full size. The largest size available will be needed for the full-grown Cane Corso.

BEDDING

A soft lambswool crate pad and perhaps a small blanket in the dog's crate will help him feel more at home. First, these things will take the place of the leaves, twigs, etc., that the pup would use in the wild to make a den; the pup can make his own "burrow" in the crate. Although your pup is

far removed from his den-making ancestors, the denning instinct is still a part of his genetic makeup. Second, until you take your pup home, he has been sleeping amid the warmth of his mother and littermates, and while a blanket is not the same as a warm, breathing body, it still provides heat and something with which to snuggle. You will want to wash your pup's bedding frequently in case he has a potty accident in his crate, and replace or remove any blanket or padding that becomes ragged and starts to fall apart.

TOYS

Toys are a must for dogs of all ages, especially for curious playful pups. Puppies are the "children" of the dog world, and what child does not love toys? Chew toys provide enjoyment for both dog and owner—your dog will enjoy playing with his favorite toys, while you will enjoy the fact that they distract him from chewing on your expensive shoes and leather sofa. Puppies love to chew; in fact, chewing is a physical need for pups as they are teething, and everything looks appetizing! The full range of your possessions—from old dishcloth to Oriental carpet—are fair game in the eyes of a teething pup. Puppies are not all that discerning when it comes to finding something literally to "sink their teeth into"— everything tastes great!

Some Cane Corsi can be chewers, especially if allowed to become bored. Being a large, strong breed, they are capable of doing a lot of damage. Cane Corsi enjoy safe marrowbones and other durable chews such as hard nylon bones. All bones and chews must be very carefully selected so that they do not splinter. They should be durable enough to withstand the Cane's strong teeth and jaws, and should always be disposed of when they show any sign of becoming dangerous. Be careful with rawhide chews, which can turn into pieces that are easy to swallow and become a mushy mess on your carpet.

A successful steal! This young Cane is more interested in his master's shoe than a chew toy, and he returns to his den with his prize.

On that note, breeders advise owners to resist stuffed toys, because they can become de-stuffed in no time. The overly excited pup may ingest the stuffing, which is neither nutritious nor digestible. Similarly, squeaky toys are quite popular, but must be avoided for the Cane Corso. Perhaps a squeaky toy can be used as an aid in training, but not for free play. If a pup "disembowels" one of these, the small plastic squeaker inside can be dangerous if swallowed. You can be sure that a Cane's strong teeth and jaws can destroy a soft toy in short order! Again, monitor the condition of all of your Cane's toys carefully and get rid of any that have been chewed to the point of becoming potentially dangerous.

LARGE BREED, LARGE TOYS

When selecting toys and chews for a Cane Corso, be sure that they are not too small. This breed has a large mouth and there is always a danger that small objects, or pieces broken off from larger toys and chew sticks, may be swallowed.

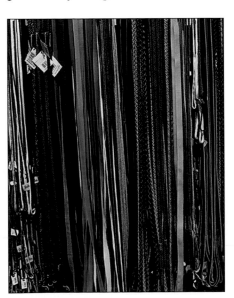

LEAD

A nylon lead is probably the best option, as it is the most resistant to puppy teeth should your pup take a liking to chewing on his lead. Of course, this is a habit that should be nipped in the bud, but, if your pup likes to chew on his lead, he has a very slim chance of being able to chew through the strong nylon. Nylon leads are also lightweight, which is good for a young Cane Corso who is just getting used to the idea of walking on a lead.

For everyday walking and safety purposes, the nylon lead is

Select a sturdy lead for your Cane. A lightweight yet strong nylon lead will be suitable for the puppy, and you will need to purchase heavier leads as the dog grows in size and strength.

wearing the collar, but soon he will not even notice that it is there. Choke collars are made for training, but should only be used by those who know exactly how to use them.

FOOD AND WATER BOWLS

Your pup will need two bowls, one for food and one for water. You may want two sets of bowls, one for indoors and one for outdoors, depending on where the dog will be fed and where he will be spending time. Stainless steel or sturdy plastic bowls are popular choices. Plastic bowls are more chewable, but dogs tend not to chew on the steel variety, which can be sterilized. It is important to buy sturdy bowls since anything is in danger of

Purchase a collar that can be adjusted as the dog grows, making sure it fits comfortably. Your Cane should become accustomed to wearing it in no time!

a good choice. As your pup grows up, and becomes larger and stronger, you will need to get a stronger lead as well.

COLLAR
Your pup should get used to wearing a collar all the time since you will want to attach his ID tags to it; plus, you have to attach the lead to something! A lightweight nylon collar is a good choice. Make certain that the collar fits snugly enough so that the pup cannot wriggle out of it, but is loose enough so that it will not be uncomfortably tight around the pup's neck. You should be able to fit a finger between the pup's neck and the collar. It may take some time for your pup to get used to

FINANCIAL RESPONSIBILITY
Grooming tools, collars, leashes, a crate, a dog bed and, of course, toys will be expenses to you when you first obtain your pup, and the cost will continue throughout your dog's lifetime. If your puppy damages or destroys your possessions (as most puppies surely will!) or something belonging to a neighbor, you can calculate additional expense. There is also flea and pest control, which every dog owner faces more than once. You must be able to handle the financial responsibility of owning a dog.

CHOOSE AN APPROPRIATE COLLAR

The **BUCKLE COLLAR** Is the standard collar used for everyday purposes. Be sure that you adjust the buckle on growing puppies. Check it every day. It can become too tight overnight! These collars can be made of leather or nylon. Attach your dog's identification tags to this collar.

The **CHOKE COLLAR** is designed for training. It is constructed of highly polished steel so that it slides easily through the stainless steel loop. The idea is that the dog controls the pressure around his neck and he will stop pulling if the collar becomes uncomfortable. It should *never* be left on a dog when not training.

The **HALTER** is for a trained dog that has to be restrained to prevent running away, chasing a cat and the like. Considered the most humane of all collars, it is frequently used on smaller dogs on which collars are not comfortable.

Select large, durable, easily cleaned bowls for your Cane Corso. Also necessary are stands on which to elevate the bowls; these should be considered mandatory accessories in order to protect your Cane from the potentially fatal bloat.

being chewed by puppy teeth and you do not want your dog to be constantly chewing apart his bowl (for his safety and for your wallet!).

As previously mentioned, the Cane Corso is susceptible to bloat. To prevent this deadly condition from affecting your dog, you should consider the purchase of bowl stands mandatory. By elevating food and water to the dog's level, he does not have to crane his neck to reach them. This provides a more natural position, aiding digestion and preventing him from swallowing air, thus reducing the risk of bloat.

CLEANING SUPPLIES

Until a pup is house-trained, you will be doing a lot of cleaning. "Accidents" will occur, which is acceptable in the beginning stages of toilet training because the puppy does not know any better. All you can do is be prepared to clean up any accidents as soon as they happen. Old towels, paper towels, newspapers and a safe disinfectant are good to have on hand.

BEYOND THE BASICS

The items previously discussed are the bare necessities. You will find out what else you need as you go along—grooming supplies, flea/tick protection, baby gates to partition a room, etc. These things will vary depending on your situation, but it is important that right away you have everything you need to feed and make your Cane Corso comfortable in his first few days at home.

PUPPY-PROOFING YOUR HOME

Aside from making sure that your Cane will be comfortable in your home, you also have to make sure that your home is safe for your Cane. This means taking precautions that your pup will not get into anything he should not get into and that there is nothing within his reach that may harm him should he sniff it, chew it, inspect it, etc. This probably seems obvious since, while you are primarily concerned with your pup's safety, at the same time you do not want your belongings to be ruined. Breakables should be placed out of reach if your dog is to have full run of the house. If he is to be limited to certain places within the house, keep any potentially dangerous items in the off-limits areas.

An electrical cord can pose a danger should the puppy decide to taste it—and who is going to convince a pup that it would not make a great chew toy? All cords and wires should be fastened tightly against the wall to keep them away from puppy teeth. If your dog is going to spend time in a crate, make sure that there is nothing near his crate that he can reach if he sticks his curious

It is your responsibility to clean up after your dog has relieved himself. Pet shops have various aids to assist in the cleanup job.

little nose or paws through the openings. Just as you would with a child, keep all household cleaners and chemicals where the pup cannot reach them; antifreeze is especially dangerous to dogs.

It is also important to make sure that the outside of your home is safe. Of course, your puppy should never be unsupervised, but a pup let loose in the yard will want to run and explore, and he should be granted that freedom. Do not let a fence give you a false sense of security; you would be surprised at how crafty (and persistent) a dog can be in figuring out how to dig under and squeeze his way through small holes, or to jump or climb over a fence.

The agile Cane Corso is certainly capable of jumping, and some will also climb and dig. The remedy is to make the fence well embedded into the ground and high enough so that it really is impossible for your dog to get over it (at least 6 feet is essential). Be sure to secure any gaps in the fence. Check the fence periodically to ensure that it is in good shape and make repairs as needed; a very determined pup may return to the same spot to "work on it" until he is able to get through.

With a large and powerful breed like the Cane, extra precautions must be taken to ensure that his area is secure and escape-proof. Your dog will want to give you a big hug for being so concerned for his safety!

HOW VACCINES WORK

If you've just bought a puppy, you surely know the importance of having your pup vaccinated, but do you understand how vaccines work? Vaccines contain the same bacteria or viruses that cause the disease you want to prevent, but they have been chemically modified so that they don't cause any harm. Instead, the vaccine causes your dog to produce antibodies that fight the harmful bacteria. Thus, if your dog is exposed to the disease in the future, the antibodies will destroy the viruses or bacteria.

FIRST TRIP TO THE VET

You have selected your puppy, and your home and family are ready. Now all you have to do is collect your Cane Corso from the breeder and the fun begins, right? Well…not so fast. Something else you need to plan is your pup's first trip to the veterinarian. Perhaps the breeder can recommend someone in the area with experience with the Cane Corso or molosser breeds, or maybe you know some other dog owners who can suggest a good vet. Either way, you should have an appointment arranged for your pup before you pick him up.

The pup's first visit will consist of an overall examination to make sure that the pup does not have any problems that are not apparent to you. The vet will also set up a schedule for the pup's vaccinations; the breeder will inform you of which ones the pup has already received and the vet can continue from there.

INTRODUCTION TO THE FAMILY

Everyone in the house will be excited about the puppy's coming home and will want to pet him and play with him, but it is best to make the introductions low-key so as not to overwhelm the puppy. He is apprehensive already. It is the first time he has been separated from his mother and the breeder, and the ride to your home is likely to be the first time he has been in a car. The last thing you want to do is smother him, as this will only frighten him further. This is not to say that human contact is not extremely necessary at this stage, because this is the time when a connection between the pup and his human family is formed. Gentle petting and soothing words should help console him, as well as just putting him down and letting him explore on his own (under your watchful eye, of course).

The pup may approach the family members or may busy himself with exploring for a while. Gradually, each person should spend some time with the pup, one at a time, crouching down to get as close to the pup's level as possible while letting him

TEMPERAMENT COUNTS
Your selection of a good puppy can be determined by your needs. A show potential or a good pet? It is your choice. Every puppy, however, should be of good temperament. Although show-quality puppies are bred and raised with emphasis on physical conformation, responsible breeders strive for equally good temperament. Do not buy from a breeder who concentrates solely on physical beauty at the expense of personality.

sniff each person's hands and petting him gently. He definitely needs human attention and he needs to be touched—this is how to form an immediate bond. Just remember that the pup is experiencing many things for the first time, at the same time. There are new people, new noises, new smells and new things to investigate, so be gentle, be affectionate and be as comforting as you can.

PUP'S FIRST NIGHT HOME

You have traveled home with your new charge safely in his crate. He's been to the vet for a thorough check-up; he's been weighed, his papers have been examined and perhaps he's even been vaccinated and wormed as well. He's met the whole family, including the excited children and the less-than-happy cat. He's explored his area, his new bed, the yard and anywhere else he's been permitted. He's eaten his first meal at home and relieved himself in the proper place. He's heard lots of new sounds, smelled new friends and seen more of the outside world than ever before...and that was just the first day! He's worn out and is ready for bed...or so you think!

It's puppy's first night home and you are ready to say "Good night." Keep in mind that this is his first night ever to be sleeping alone. His dam and littermates are no longer at paw's length and he's a bit scared, cold and lonely. Be reassuring to your new family member, but this is not the time to spoil him and give in to his inevitable whining.

Puppies whine. They whine to let others know where they are and hopefully to get company out of it. Place your pup in his new bed or crate in his designated area and close the door. Mercifully, he may fall asleep without a peep. When the inevitable occurs, however, ignore the whining—he is fine. Be strong and keep his interest in mind. Do not allow yourself to feel guilty and visit the pup. He will fall asleep eventually.

Many breeders recommend placing a piece of bedding from the pup's former home in his new bed so that he recognizes and is comforted by the scent of his littermates. Others still advise placing a hot water bottle in the bed for warmth. The latter may be

TIME TO GO HOME

Breeders rarely release puppies until they are eight to ten weeks of age. This is an acceptable age for most breeds of dog, excepting Toy breeds, which are not released until around 12 weeks, given their petite sizes. If a breeder has a puppy that is 12 weeks of age or older, he is likely well social-ized and house-trained. Be sure that he is otherwise healthy before deciding to take him home.

a good idea provided the pup doesn't attempt to suckle—he'll get good and wet, and may not fall asleep so fast.

Puppy's first night can be somewhat stressful for both the pup and his new family. Remember that you are setting the tone of nighttime at your house. Unless you want to play with your pup every night at 10 p.m., midnight and 2 a.m., don't initiate the habit. Your family will thank you, and soon so will your pup!

PREVENTING PUPPY PROBLEMS

SOCIALIZATION

Now that you have done all of the preparatory work and have helped your pup get accustomed to his new home and family, it is about time for you to have some fun! Socializing your Cane Corso pup gives you the opportunity to show off your new friend, and your pup gets to reap the benefits of being

A Cane is a girl's best friend! A properly bred and typical Cane Corso is even-tempered, dependable and trustworthy around his young friends, and children should treat the dog with care and respect.

an adorable intriguing creature that people will want to pet and, in general, think is just irresistible.

Besides getting to know his new family, your puppy should be exposed to other people, animals and situations. This will help him become well adjusted as he grows up and less prone to being timid or fearful of the new things he will encounter. Remember that a Cane Corso will not look for a fight, but will most certainly stand his ground if challenged and will not back down. Cane Corsi are dominant toward other dogs, so your early socialization efforts are essential. Of course, your puppy must not come into close contact with dogs you don't know well until his course of injections is fully complete.

Your pup's socialization began with the breeder, but now it is your responsibility to continue it; socialization is a major concern in this breed. The socialization your

---

SETTLE DOWN!

It is important that a Cane Corso is not allowed to get overexcited during play. If this happens in puppyhood, your puppy must be calmed down immediately; this is a lesson that must be taught early on. Owners must always keep in mind that a full-grown Cane can cause unintentional harm if allowed to engage in rough games.

NATURAL TOXINS

Examine your grass and landscaping before bringing your puppy home. Many varieties of plants have leaves, stems or flowers that are toxic if ingested, and you can depend on a curious puppy to investigate them.

If you see your dog carrying a piece of vegetation in his mouth, approach him in a quiet, disinterested manner, avoid eye contact, pet him and gradually remove the plant from his mouth. Alternatively, offer him a treat and maybe he'll drop the plant on his own accord. Be sure no toxic plants are growing in your own yard or kept in your home. Ask your vet for information on poisonous plants or research them at your library.

Cane receives until the age of 12 weeks is the most critical, as this is the time when he forms his impressions of the outside world. Be especially careful during the eight-to-ten-week-old period, also known as the fear period. The interaction he receives during this time should be gentle and reassuring. Lack of socialization, and/or negative experiences during the socialization period, can manifest itself in fear and aggression as the dog grows up. Your puppy needs lots of positive interaction, which of course includes human contact, affection, handling and exposure to other animals.

Once your pup has received his necessary vaccinations, feel free to take him out and about (on his lead, of course). Walk him around the neighborhood, take him on your daily errands, let people pet him, let him meet other dogs and pets, etc. Puppies do not have to try to make friends; there will be no shortage of people who will want to introduce themselves. Just make sure that you carefully supervise each meeting.

If the neighborhood children want to say hello, for example, that is great—children and pups most often make great companions. However, sometimes an excited child can unintentionally handle a pup too roughly, or an overzealous pup can playfully nip a little too hard. You want to make socialization experiences positive ones. What a pup learns during this very formative stage will affect his attitude toward future encounters. You want your dog to be comfortable around everyone. A pup that has a bad experience with a child may grow up to be a dog that is shy around or aggressive toward children.

CONSISTENCY IN TRAINING

Dogs, being pack animals, naturally need a leader, or else they try to establish dominance in their packs. When you welcome a dog into your family, the choice of who becomes the leader and who becomes the pack is entirely up to you! Your Cane's intuitive quest for dominance, coupled with the fact that it is nearly impossible to look at an adorable Cane Corso pup with his "puppy-dog" eyes and not cave in, give the pup almost an unfair advantage in getting the upper hand! A pup will definitely test the waters to see what he can and cannot do.

Do not give in to those pleading eyes—stand your ground when it comes to disciplining the pup and make sure that all family members do the same. It will only confuse the pup if Mother tells him to get off the sofa when he is used to sitting up there with Father to watch the nightly news. Avoid discrepancies by having all members of the household decide

on the rules before the pup even comes home...and be consistent in enforcing them! Early training shapes the dog's personality, so you cannot be unclear in what you expect

COMMON PUPPY PROBLEMS

The best way to prevent puppy problems is to be proactive in stopping an undesirable behavior as soon as it starts. The old saying "You can't teach an old dog new

MANNERS MATTER

During the socialization process, a puppy should meet people, experience different environments and definitely be exposed to other canines. Through playing and interacting with other dogs, your puppy will learn lessons, ranging from controlling the pressure of his jaws by biting his littermates to the inner-workings of the canine pack that he will apply to his relationships with humans and other animals for the rest of his life. That is why removing a puppy from the litter too early (before eight weeks) can be detrimental to the pup's development.

DEALING WITH PROBLEMS

The majority of problems that are commonly seen in young pups will disappear as your dog gets older. However, how you deal with problems when he is young will determine how he reacts to discipline as an adult dog. It is important to establish who is boss (ideally it will be you!) right away when you are first bonding with your dog. This bond will set the tone for the rest of your life together. If you have a puppy that seems untrainable, take him to a trainer or behaviorist. The dog may have a personality problem that requires the help of a professional, or perhaps you need help in learning how to train your dog.

wait until the pup's bad behavior becomes the adult dog's bad habit. There are some problems that are especially prevalent in puppies as they develop.

NIPPING

As puppies start to teethe, they feel the need to sink their teeth into anything available...unfortunately, that usually includes your fingers, arms, hair and toes. You may find this behavior cute for the first five seconds...until you feel just how sharp those puppy teeth are. Nipping is something you want to discourage immediately and consistently with a firm "No!" (or whatever number of firm "Nos" it takes for him to understand that you mean business). Then, replace your finger with an appropriate chew toy. While this behavior is merely annoying when the dog is young, it can become dangerous as your Cane's adult teeth grow in and his jaws develop, as this is a breed that grows very strong. Your Cane does not mean any harm with a friendly nip, but he also does not know his own strength.

CRYING/WHINING

Your pup will often cry, whine, whimper, howl or make some type of commotion when he is left alone. This is basically his way of calling out for attention to make sure that you know he is

tricks" does not necessarily hold true, but it *is* true that it is much easier to discourage bad behavior in a young developing pup than to there and that you have not forgotten about him. Your puppy feels insecure when he is left alone, when you are out of the house and he is in his crate or when you are in another part of the house and he cannot see you. The noise he is making is an expression of the anxiety he feels at being alone, so he needs to be taught that being alone is okay. You are not actually training the dog to stop making noise; rather, you are training him to feel comfortable when he is alone and thus removing the need for him to make the noise.

This is where the crate with cozy bedding and a toy comes in handy. You want to know that your pup is safe when you are not there to supervise, and you know that he will be safe in his crate rather than roaming freely about the house. In order for the pup to stay in his crate without making a fuss, he first needs to be comfortable in his crate. On that note, it is extremely important that the crate is never used as a form of punishment; this will cause the pup to view the crate as a negative place, rather than as a place of his own for safety and retreat.

Accustom the pup to the crate in short, gradually increasing time intervals in which you put him in the crate, maybe with a treat, and stay in the room with him. If he cries or makes a fuss, do not go to him, but stay in his sight. Gradually he will realize that staying in his crate is all right without your help, and it will not be so traumatic for him when you are not around. Remember never to confine your pup for more than two hours, unless he is sleeping.

CHEWING TIPS

Chewing goes hand in hand with nipping in the sense that a teething puppy is always looking for a way to soothe his aching gums. In this case, instead of chewing on you, he may have taken a liking to your favorite shoe or something else that he should not be chewing. Again, realize that this is a normal canine behavior that does not need to be discouraged, only redirected. Your pup just needs to be taught what is acceptable to chew on and what is off-limits. Consistently tell him "No!" when you catch him chewing on something forbidden and give him a chew toy.

Conversely, praise him when you catch him chewing on something appropriate. In this way, you are discouraging the inappropriate behavior and reinforcing the desired behavior. The puppy's chewing should stop after his adult teeth have come in, but an adult dog continues to chew for various reasons—perhaps because he is bored, needs to relieve tension or just likes to chew. That is why it is important to redirect his chewing when he is still young.

FEEDING CONSIDERATIONS

When you buy your puppy, the breeder should provide you with a diet sheet that details exactly how your puppy has been fed. Of course, you will be at liberty to change that food, together with the frequency and timing of meals, as the youngster reaches adulthood, but this should be done gradually.

Cane Corsi are not especially difficult to feed, but care should be taken that pups are not allowed to put on too much weight too quickly. A carefully selected breeder should be able to give good advice regarding the diet that has suited his own dogs best.

Most Cane Corso owners like to feed two small meals per day, rather than just one larger one. Giving treats between meals should be done with care. As everyone knows, too many treats can all too easily lead to obesity. Smaller, regular meals are especially useful for older dogs, and in a breed like that Cane that can suffer from gastric torsion (bloat), avoidance of meals that are too large and heavy is always wise. It is absolutely essential to remember to elevate your dog's bowls and that no Cane Corso should ever be fed within at least an hour of strenuous exercise. Many owners prefer to leave a two-hour gap.

There are now numerous high-quality canine dog foods available, and one of them is likely to suit your own dog. Of

STORING DOG FOOD

You must store your dry dog food carefully. Open packages of dog food quickly lose their vitamin value, usually within 90 days of being opened. Mold spores and vermin could also contaminate the food.

course, plenty of fresh water should always be available, and this is especially important if feeding a complete (commercial) dry food. When a Cane Corso has reached maturity, many breeders like to lower the protein content, and it is generally accepted that a lower protein content is more suitable once a dog has begun to lead a more sedentary life.

Some owners prefer to feed a canned food with mixer, instead of the even more convenient complete dry-food diets, many of which are carefully and scientifically balanced. A lot will depend on personal preference, and indeed there are owners who like to feed fresh food. If giving a fresh diet, care should of course be taken not to feed any meats with bones. Cane Corsi, though, can cope well with safe, large marrowbones. These seem to provide great pleasure and also help to keep teeth in good condition, but they must always be checked for splinters and carefully removed when they begin to get worn down.

If you choose to feed a complete commercial food, the choices for your Cane are many and varied. There are simply dozens of brands of food in all sorts of flavors and textures, ranging from puppy diets to those for seniors. There are even hypoallergenic and low-calorie diets available. Because your Cane

FOOD PREFERENCE

Selecting the best dry dog food is difficult. There is no majority consensus among veterinary scientists as to the value of nutrient analysis (protein, fat, fiber, moisture, ash, cholesterol, minerals, etc.). All agree that feeding trials are what matter most, but you also have to consider the individual dog. The dog's weight, age and activity level, and what pleases his taste, all must be considered. It is probably best to take the advice of your veterinarian. Every dog has individual dietary requirements, and should be fed accordingly.

If your dog is fed a good dry food, he does not require supplements of meat or vegetables. Dogs do appreciate a little variety in their diets, so you may choose to stay with the same brand but vary the flavor. Alternatively, you may wish to add a little flavored stock to give a difference to the taste.

FEEDING TIPS

- Dog food must be served at room temperature, neither too hot nor too cold. Fresh water, changed often and served in a clean bowl, is mandatory.
- Never feed your dog from the table while you are eating, and never feed your dog leftovers from your own meal. They usually contain too much fat and too much seasoning.
- Dogs must chew their food. Hard pellets are excellent; soups and stews are to be avoided.
- Don't add leftovers or any extras to a complete commercial dog food. The normal food is usually balanced, and adding something extra destroys the balance.
- Except for age-related changes, dogs do not require dietary variations. They can be fed the same diet, day after day, without their becoming bored or ill.

Corso's food has a bearing on coat, health and temperament, it is essential that the most suitable diet is selected for a dog of his age. It is fair to say, however, that even experienced owners can be perplexed by the enormous range of foods available. Only understanding what is best for your dog will help you reach an informed decision.

Dog foods are produced in three basic types: dry, semi-moist and canned. Dry foods are useful for the cost-conscious, for overall they tend to be less expensive than semi-moist or canned foods. Dry foods also contain the least fat and the most preservatives. In general, canned foods are made up of 60–70% water, while semi-moist ones often contain so much sugar that they are perhaps the least preferred by owners, even though their dogs seem to like them. When selecting your dog's diet, three stages of development must be considered: the puppy stage, the adult stage and the senior stage.

Puppy Stage

Puppies instinctively want to suck milk from their mother's teats; a normal puppy will exhibit this behavior just a few moments following birth. If puppies do not attempt to suckle within the first half-hour or so, they should be encouraged to do so by placing them on the nipples, having selected ones with plenty of milk. This early milk supply is important in providing the essential colostrum, which protects the puppies during the first eight to ten weeks of their lives. Although a mother's milk is much better than any commercially prepared milk formula, despite there being some excellent ones available, if the puppies do not feed, the breeder will have to feed them by hand. For those with less experience, advice from a vet is

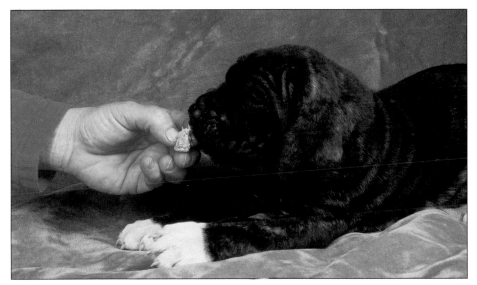

All puppies welcome treats, but don't overdo it. Never mistake too much food for extra nutrition, especially with a rapidly growing breed where overfeeding can cause skeletal problems.

important so that not only the right quantity of milk is fed but also that of correct quality, fed at suitably frequent intervals, usually every two hours during the first few days of life.

Puppies should be allowed to nurse from their mother for about the first six weeks, although, starting around the third or fourth week, the breeder will begin to introduce small portions of suitable solid food. Most breeders like to introduce alternate milk and meat meals initially, building up to weaning time.

By the time the puppies are seven or a maximum of eight weeks old, they should be fully weaned and fed solely on a proprietary puppy food. Selection of the most suitable, good-quality diet at this time is essential, for a puppy's

fastest growth rate is during the first year of life. Vets and breeders are usually able to offer advice in this regard. The frequency of meals will be reduced over time, and the young Cane can be kept on the same type of food until around 9 to 12 months old, depending on the dog. Although most puppy and junior diets should be well balanced for the needs of your dog, owners should consult their breeder about additional vitamins,

TEST FOR PROPER DIET
A good test for proper diet is the color, odor and firmness of your dog's stool. A healthy dog usually produces three semi-hard stools per day. The stools should have no unpleasant odor. They should be the same color from excretion to excretion.

minerals and proteins. Calcium supplementation is commonly prescribed for growing dogs.

ADULT DIETS

A Cane Corso will usually have reached maximum height by 15 to 18 months, but the head and body will continue to develop for considerably longer. The time at which to switch your Cane to an adult food can vary according to the make of food used and to the individual's bodily development. Cane Corsi are generally changed to an adult diet by around 9 to 12 months of age.

Again you should rely upon your breeder, vet or dietary specialist to recommend an acceptable maintenance diet. Major dog-food manufacturers specialize in this type of food, and it is merely necessary for you to select the one best suited to your dog's needs. Active dogs have different requirements from more sedentary dogs.

SENIOR DIETS

As dogs get older, their metabolism changes. The older dog usually exercises less, moves more slowly and sleeps more. This change in lifestyle and physiological performance requires a change in diet. Since these changes take place slowly, they might not be recognizable. What is easily recognizable is weight gain. By continuing to feed your dog an adult-maintenance diet when he is slowing down metaboli-

cally, your dog will gain weight. Obesity in an older dog compounds the health problems that already accompany old age.

As your dog gets older, few of his organs function up to par. The kidneys slow down and the intestines become less efficient. These age-related factors are best handled with a change in diet and a change in feeding schedule to

THE CANINE GOURMET
Your dog does not prefer a fresh bone. Indeed, he wants it properly aged and, if given such a treat indoors, he is more likely to try to bury it in the carpet than he is to settle in for a good chew! If you have a yard, give him such delicacies outside and guide him to a place suitable for his "bone yard." He will carefully place the treasure in its earthy vault and seemingly forget about it. Trust me, his seeming distaste or lack of thanks for your thoughtfulness is not that at all. He will return in a few days to inspect the bone, perhaps to re-bury it, and when it is just right, he will relish it as much as you do that cooked-to-perfection steak. If he is in a concrete or bricked kennel run, he will be especially frustrated at the hopelessness of the situation. He will vacillate between ignoring it completely, giving it a few licks to speed the curing process with saliva, and trying to hide it behind the water bowl! When the bone has aged a bit, he will set to work on it.

give smaller portions that are more easily digested.

Some Cane Corsi never change to a senior diet, but others move over from about seven years of age. There is no single best diet for every older dog. While many dogs do well on light or senior diets, other dogs do better on puppy diets or special premium diets such as lamb and rice. Be sensitive to your senior Cane's diet, as this will help control other problems that may arise with your old friend.

WATER

Just as your dog needs proper nutrition from his food, water is an essential "nutrient" as well. Water keeps the dog's body properly hydrated and promotes normal function of the body's systems. During house-training, it is necessary to keep an eye on how much water your Cane Corso is drinking, but once he is reliably trained he should have access to clean fresh water at all times. Keep in mind that your Cane should never be allowed to gulp water, especially at mealtimes. Make certain that the dog's water bowl is clean and elevated. Change the water often because Cane Corsi do not like the taste of drool in their water and will refuse to drink.

EXERCISE

Cane Corsi need plenty of exercise but, just like with most larger, heavy breeds, they should not be

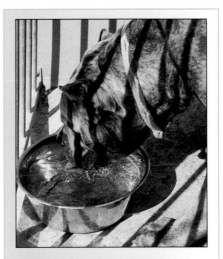

DRINK, DRANK, DRUNK— MAKE IT A DOUBLE

In both humans and dogs, as well as other living organisms, water forms the major part of nearly every body tissue. Naturally, we take water for granted, but without it, life as we know it would cease.

For dogs, water is needed to keep their bodies functioning biochemically. Additionally, water is needed to replace the water lost while panting. Unlike humans, who are able to sweat to dissipate heat, dogs must pant to cool down, thereby losing the vital water that their bodies need to regulate their body temperatures. Humans lose electrolyte-containing products and other body-fluid components through sweating; dogs do not lose anything except water.

Water is essential always, but especially so when the weather is hot or humid or when your dog is exercising or working vigorously.

engaged in strenuous play as youngsters. Cane Corso puppies should not be over-exercised during the crucial period of bone growth; however, they should be allowed some free running in a suitably safe area. Having said that, training the basic commands is absolutely essential from an early age.

In adulthood, plenty of exercise is essential to keep the dog's muscles in tone, and walking up and down a gradient will be of special help in this regard. A combination of exercise on both hard and soft surfaces will help to keep toenails trimmed and feet in tight condition.

Free runs should, of course, only be allowed in places that are completely safe. All possible escape routes should be thoroughly checked out and secured before letting the dog off-lead. After exercise, Cane Corsi should be allowed to settle down quietly for a rest, and please remember that, following exercise, plenty of time must be allowed before feeding.

Bear in mind that an overweight dog should never be suddenly over-exercised; instead, he should be encouraged to increase exercise slowly. Also keep in mind that not only is exercise essential to keep the dog's body fit, it is essential to his mental well-being. A bored dog will find something to do, which

> ## "DOES THIS COLLAR MAKE ME LOOK FAT?"
> While humans may obsess about how they look and how trim their bodies are, many people believe that extra weight on their dogs is a good thing. The truth is, pets should not be over- or under-weight, as both can lead to or signal sickness. In order to tell how fit your pet is, run your hands over his ribs. Are his ribs buried under a layer of fat or are they sticking out consider-ably? If your pet is within his normal weight range, you should be able to feel the ribs easily, but they should not protrude abnormally. If you stand above him, the outline of his body should resemble an hourglass. Some breeds do tend to be leaner while some are a bit stockier, but making sure your dog is the right weight for his breed will certainly contribute to his good health.

often manifests itself in some type of destructive behavior. In this sense, exercise is just as essential for the owner's mental well-being!

GROOMING

BRUSHING
Although the Cane Corso is a short-coated breed, some grooming is essential to keep the coat in good, healthy, clean condition. Every owner will have his own preference as to

what equipment suits best. This may be a combination of grooming gloves, chamois leathers, pure bristle brushes and rubber brushes. It is wise to get into the routine of grooming regularly, ideally short sessions on a daily basis. Regular and thorough grooming during times of shedding is a must.

A Cane Corso that has become wet when exercising in the rain should always be wiped down thoroughly with a towel, so as not to remain damp, with special attention being paid to the dog's underside. Provided the coat is well cared for, Cane Corsi only need baths occasionally.

BATHING

Dogs do not need to be bathed nearly as often as humans do, but bathing as needed is important for healthy skin and a clean, shiny coat. Again, like most anything, if

Everyone in the family can help accustom the pup to his routine brushing. This type of interaction builds the bond between dog and child, but of course children and pups should always be supervised when spending time together.

SOAP IT UP

The use of human soap products like shampoo, bubble bath and hand soap can be damaging to a dog's coat and skin. Human products are too strong; they remove the protective oils coating the dog's hair and skin that make him water-resistant. Use only shampoo made especially for dogs. You may like to use a medicated shampoo, which will help to keep external parasites at bay.

you accustom your pup to being bathed as a puppy, it will be second nature by the time he grows up. You want your dog to be at ease in the bath or else it could end up a wet, soapy, messy ordeal for both of you!

Brush your Cane Corso thoroughly before wetting his coat. This will get rid of most dead hair and debris, which are harder to remove when the coat is wet. Make certain that your dog has a good non-slip surface on which to stand. Begin by wetting the dog's coat, checking the water

Cane Corsi do not require sophisticated grooming equipment. You can obtain the basics from your pet-supply store to keep your Cane's coat looking its shiny best.

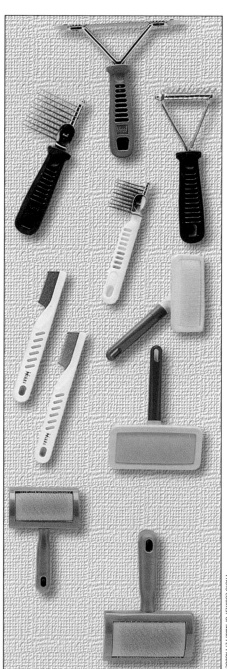

GROOMING EQUIPMENT

Always purchase quality grooming equipment so that your tools will last for many years to come. Here are some basics:

• Bristle brush
• Grooming glove
• Rubber mat
• Dog shampoo
• Spray hose attachment
• Towels
• Ear cleaner
• Cotton balls
• Nail clippers
• Dental-care products

temperature to make sure that it is neither too hot nor too cold. A shower or hose attachment is necessary for thoroughly wetting and rinsing the coat.

Next, apply shampoo to the dog's coat and work it into a good lather. Wash the head last, as you do not want shampoo to drip into the dog's eyes while you are washing the rest of his body. You should use only a shampoo that is made for dogs. Do not use a product made for human hair. Work the shampoo all the way down to the skin. You can use this opportunity to check the skin for any bumps, bites or other abnormalities. Do not neglect any area of the body—get all of the hard-to-reach places.

Once the dog has been thoroughly shampooed, he requires an equally thorough rinsing. Shampoo left in the coat can be irritating to the dog's skin. Protect his eyes from the shampoo by shielding them with your hand and directing the flow of water in the opposite direction. You also should avoid getting water in the ear canal. Be prepared for your Cane to shake out his coat—you might want to stand back, but make sure you have a hold on the dog to keep him from running through the house and leaving a wet trail! Have a towel ready.

EAR CLEANING

The ears should be kept clean with a soft cotton ball or pad, and an ear-cleaning powder or liquid made for dogs. Never probe into the ear canal with anything, as this can cause injury. Be on the lookout for any signs of infection or ear-mite infestation. If your Cane Corso has been shaking his head or scratching at his ears frequently, this usually indicates a problem. If the dog's ears have an unusual odor, this is a sure sign of mite infestation or infection, and a signal to have his ears checked by the vet.

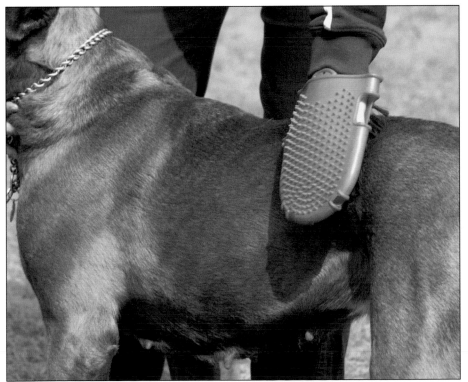

A grooming glove or mitt is a handy tool that makes your Cane's routine once-overs easy for you and pleasant for the dog. Many dogs grow to like the feel of being brushed with this type of implement.

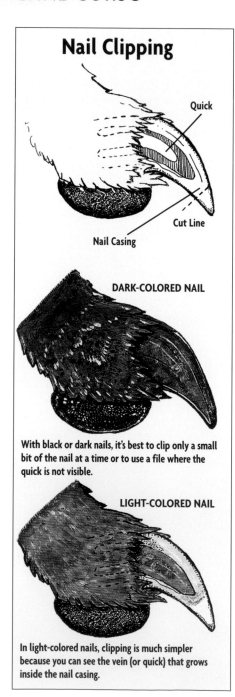

Nail Clipping

Quick

Cut Line

Nail Casing

DARK-COLORED NAIL

With black or dark nails, it's best to clip only a small bit of the nail at a time or to use a file where the quick is not visible.

LIGHT-COLORED NAIL

In light-colored nails, clipping is much simpler because you can see the vein (or quick) that grows inside the nail casing.

Also be on the lookout for grass seeds and the like becoming trapped in the ear. These can cause untold damage if they are allowed to work their way down to the inner ear, when veterinary attention will become necessary.

NAIL CLIPPING

Your Cane Corso should be accustomed to having his nails trimmed at an early age, since nail clipping will be a part of your maintenance routine throughout his life. A dog's long nails can scratch someone unintentionally and also have a better chance of ripping and bleeding, or causing the feet to spread. How frequently the nails will need to be clipped will depend on how much the dog walks on hard surfaces, but they should be checked on a weekly basis. A good rule of thumb is that if you can hear your dog's nails' clicking on the floor when he walks, his nails are too long.

Before you start cutting, make sure you can identify the "quick" in each nail. The quick is a blood vessel that runs through the center of each nail and grows rather close to the end. The quick will bleed if accidentally cut, which will be quite painful for the dog as it contains nerve endings. Keep some type of clotting agent on hand, such as a styptic pencil or styptic powder (the type used for shaving). This

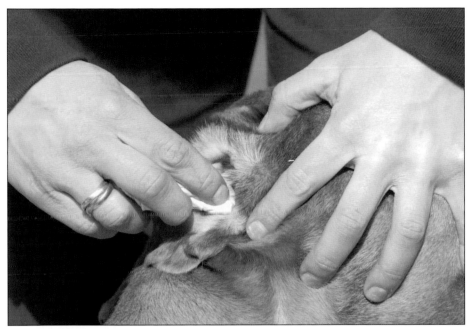

Clean the outer part of the ears with a soft cloth or piece of soft cotton. Never delve deeper than you can see, as probing into the ear can be dangerous for the dog.

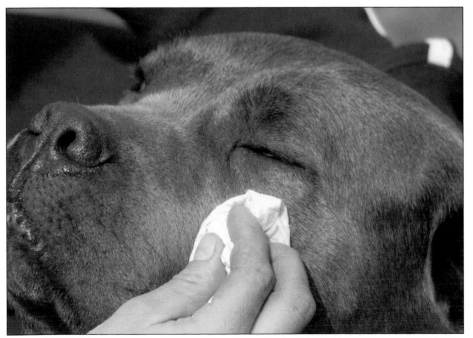

The area around the eyes can be cleaned gently as needed with a soft wipe and cleansing product made for this purpose.

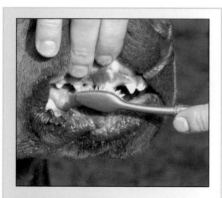

DEADLY DECAY
Did you know that periodontal disease (a condition of the bone and gums surrounding a tooth) can be fatal? Having your dog's teeth and mouth checked yearly along with making home dental-care part of your regular routine can prevent it.

will stop the bleeding quickly when applied to the end of the cut nail. Do not panic if you cut the quick, just stop the bleeding and talk soothingly to your dog. Once he has calmed down, move on to the next nail. It is better to clip a little at a time, particularly with black-nailed dogs.

Hold your pup steady as you begin trimming his nails; you do not want him to make any sudden movements or run away. Talk to him soothingly and stroke him as you clip. Holding his foot in your hand, simply take off the end of each nail with one swift clip. You should purchase nail clippers that are made for use on dogs; you can

probably find them wherever you buy pet or grooming supplies.

TOOTH CARE
Teeth should always be kept as free from tartar as possible, and cleaning your dog's teeth at home can be incorporated into your grooming routine. Weekly brushing will keep your Cane's teeth clean and strong, while preventing gum disease and "doggy" breath. There are now tooth-cleaning products made for dogs, including the basics like toothbrushes and canine toothpaste.

TRAVELING WITH YOUR DOG

ROAD TRAVEL
You should accustom your Cane Corso to riding in a car at an early age. You may or may not take him in the car often, but at the very least he will need to go to the vet and you do not want these trips to be traumatic for the dog or troublesome for you. The safest way for a dog to ride in the car is in his crate. If he uses a crate in the house, you can use the same crate for travel, provided you have a Cane-sized vehicle.

Put the pup in the crate and see how he reacts. If he seems uneasy, you can have a passenger hold him on his lap while you drive. Another option for car travel is a specially made safety harness for dogs, which straps the dog in much like a seat belt. Owners of large vehicles like sport utility vehicles or station wagons can install partitions to create an area of safe confinement in the rear of the vehicle. Regardless of which option you choose, do not let the dog roam loose in the vehicle—this is very dangerous! If you should stop short, your dog can be thrown and injured. If the dog starts climbing on you and pestering you while you are driving, you will not be able to concentrate on the road. It is an unsafe situation for everyone—human and canine.

For long trips, bring along some water and be prepared to stop to let the dog relieve himself. Take with you whatever you need to clean up after him, including some paper towels and perhaps some old rags for use should he have a potty accident in the car or suffer from motion sickness. As safety precautions, never leave your dog alone in the car, even for short periods, and always keep your Cane on-lead when you make stops.

AIR TRAVEL

Contact your chosen airline before proceeding with travel plans that include your Cane Corso. The dog will be required to travel in a fiberglass crate and you should always check in advance with the airline

Ready to go! This car has been made Cane-friendly by creating a safe area of confinement in the rear section of the vehicle with a partition.

regarding specific requirements for the crate's size, type and labeling, as well as any travel restrictions and necessary health certifications.

To help put the dog at ease for the trip, give him one of his favorite toys in the crate. Do not feed the dog for several hours before the trip in order to minimize his need to relieve himself. Some airlines require you to provide documentation as to

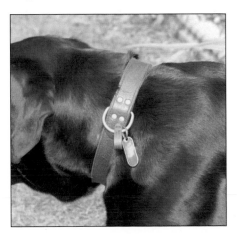

Your Cane's everyday collar should have his ID tags securely fastened to it. Your dog should be accustomed to wearing his collar at all times; this is especially important any time he is outdoors or when you are traveling.

when the dog has last been fed. In any case, a light meal is best. For long trips, you will have to attach food and water bowls to the outside of the dog's crate so that airline employees can tend to him between legs of the trip.

Make sure that your Cane is properly identified and that your contact information appears on his ID tags and on his crate. Animals travel in a different area of the airplane from human passengers, so every rule must be strictly followed so as to prevent any risk of getting separated from your dog.

VACATIONS AND BOARDING

So you want to take a family vacation—and you want to include *all* members of the

Select a boarding kennel for your Cane Corso well in advance of your needing its services. It would be helpful if the kennel is familiar with the breed, as many Cane Corsi do not do well in environments with other dogs.

family. You would probably make arrangements for accommodations ahead of time anyway, but this is especially important when traveling with a dog. You do not want to make an overnight stop at the only place around for miles, only to find out that they do not allow dogs. Also, you do not want to reserve a place for your family without confirming that you are traveling with a dog (especially a large dog!), because, if it is against the hotel's policy, you may end up without a place to stay.

Alternatively, if you are traveling and choose not to bring your Cane Corso, you will have to make arrangements for him while you are away. Some options are to take him to a familiar friend's house to stay while you are gone, to have a trusted neighbor (whom the dog knows) stop by often or stay at your house or to bring your dog to a reputable boarding kennel. If you choose to board him at a kennel, you should visit in advance to see the facilities provided and where the dogs are kept. Are the dogs' areas spacious and kept clean? Talk to some of the employees and observe how they treat the dogs—do they spend time with the dogs, play with them, exercise them, etc.? Remember that the Cane may not react well to other dogs; does the kennel have experience with the breed? Also find out the kennel's

IDENTIFICATION OPTIONS

As puppies become more and more expensive, especially those puppies of high quality for showing and/or breeding, they have a greater chance of being stolen. The usual collar dog tag is, of course, easily removed. But there are two more permanent techniques that have become widely used for identification.

The puppy microchip implantation involves the injection of a small microchip, about the size of a corn kernel, under the skin of the dog. If your dog shows up at a clinic or shelter, or is offered for resale under less-than-savory circumstances, it can be positively identified by the microchip. The microchip is scanned, and a registry quickly identifies you as the owner.

Tattooing is done on various parts of the dog, from his belly to his ears. The number tattooed can be your telephone number, your dog's registration number or any other number that you can easily memorize. When professional dog thieves see a tattooed dog, they usually lose interest. For the safety of our dogs, no laboratory facility or dog broker will accept a tattooed dog as stock.

Discuss microchipping and tattooing with your veterinarian and breeder. Some vets perform these services on their own premises for a reasonable fee. To ensure that your dog's identification is effective, be certain that the dog is then properly registered with a legitimate national database.

policy on vaccinations and what they require. This is for all of the dogs' safety, since there is a greater risk of diseases being passed from dog to dog when dogs are kept together.

IDENTIFICATION

Your Cane Corso is your valued companion and friend. That is why you always keep a close eye on him and you have made sure that he cannot escape from the yard or wriggle out of his collar and run away from you. However, accidents can happen and there may come a time when your dog unexpectedly becomes separated from you. If this unfortunate event

should occur, the first thing on your mind will be finding him. Proper identification, including an ID tag and possibly a tattoo and/or a microchip, will increase the chances of his being returned to you safely and quickly.

The light skin on the belly is a common place for a dog to be tattooed, as the tattoo is easily visible in this area.

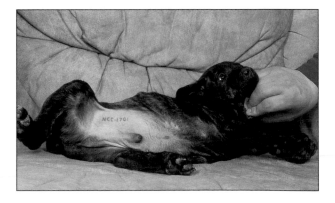

TRAINING YOUR

CANE CORSO

Living with an untrained dog is a lot like owning a piano that you do not know how to play—it is a nice object to look at, but it does not do much more than that to bring you pleasure. Now try taking piano lessons, and suddenly the piano comes alive and brings forth magical sounds and rhythms that set your heart singing and your body swaying.

The same is true with your Cane Corso. Any dog is a big responsibility and, if not trained sensibly, may develop unacceptable behavior that annoys you or could even cause family friction.

To train your Cane, you may like to enroll in an obedience class. Teach your dog good manners as you learn how and why he behaves the way he does. Find out how to communicate with your dog and how to recognize and understand his communications with you. Suddenly the dog takes on a new role in your life—he is clever, interesting, well behaved and fun to be with. He demonstrates his bond of devotion to you daily. In other words, your Cane does wonders for your ego because he constantly reminds you that you are not only his leader, you are his hero!

Those involved with teaching dog obedience and counseling owners about their dogs' behavior have discovered some interesting facts about dog ownership. For example, training dogs when they are puppies results in the highest rate of success in developing well-mannered and well-adjusted adult dogs. Training an older dog, from six months to six years of age, can produce almost equal results, providing that the owner accepts the dog's slower rate of learning capability and is willing to work patiently to help the dog succeed at developing to his fullest potential. Unfortunately, many owners of untrained adult dogs lack the patience factor, so they do not persist until their dogs are successful at learning particular behaviors.

Training a puppy aged 10 to 16 weeks (20 weeks at the most) is like working with a dry sponge

An adult dog of this size, if not trained, would be very difficult to control. Early training of the Cane Corso is essential in developing a politely behaved, reliable adult.

in a pool of water. The pup soaks up whatever you show him and constantly looks for more things to do and learn. At this early age, his body is not yet producing hormones, and therein lies the reason for such a high rate of success. Without hormones, he is focused on his owners and not particularly interested in investigating other places, dogs, people, etc. You are his leader: his provider of food, water, shelter and security. He latches onto you and wants to stay close. He will

PARENTAL GUIDANCE

Training a dog is a life experience. Many parents admit that much of what they know about raising children they learned from caring for their dogs. Dogs respond to love, fairness and guidance, just as children do. Become a good dog owner and you may become an even better parent.

usually follow you from room to room, will not let you out of his sight when you are outdoors with him and will respond in like manner to the people and animals you encounter. This is where socialization becomes a key component in your Cane's education. If you greet a friend warmly, he will be willing to greet the person as well. If, however, you are hesitant or anxious about the approach of a stranger, his suspicious nature will arise.

Once the puppy begins to produce hormones, his natural curiosity emerges and he begins to investigate the world around him. It is at this time when you may notice that the untrained dog begins to wander away from you and even ignore your commands to stay close. When this behavior becomes a problem, you have two choices: get rid of the dog or train him. It is strongly urged that you choose the latter option.

You usually will be able to find obedience classes within a reasonable distance from your home, but you can also do a lot to train your dog yourself. Sometimes there are classes available, but the tuition is too costly. Whatever the circumstances, the solution to training your dog without formal obedience classes lies within the pages of this book.

FEAR AGGRESSION

Pups who are subjected to physical abuse during training commonly end up with behavioral problems as adults. One common result of abuse is fear aggression, in which a dog will lash out, bare his teeth, snarl and finally bite someone by whom he feels threatened. For example, your daughter may be playing with the dog one afternoon. As they play hide-and-seek, she backs the dog into a corner and, as she attempts to tease him playfully, he bites her hand. Examine the cause of this behavior. Did your daughter ever hit the dog? Did someone who resembles your daughter hit or scream at the dog?

Fortunately, fear aggression is relatively easy to correct. Have your daughter engage in only positive activities with the dog, such as feeding, petting and walking. She should not give any corrections or negative feedback. If the dog still growls or cowers away from her, allow someone else to accompany them. After approximately one week, the dog should feel that he can rely on her for many positive things, and he will also be prevented from reacting fearfully towards anyone who might resemble her.

This chapter is devoted to helping you train your Cane Corso at home. If the recommended procedures are followed faithfully, you may expect positive results that will prove rewarding both to you and your dog. Whether your new charge is a puppy or a mature adult, the methods of teaching and the techniques we use in training basic behaviors are the same. After all, no dog, whether puppy or adult, likes harsh or inhumane methods. All creatures, however, respond favorably to gentle motivational methods and sincere praise and encouragement. Now let us get started.

HOUSE-TRAINING

You can train a puppy to relieve himself wherever you choose, but this must be somewhere suitable. You should bear in mind from the outset that when your puppy is old enough to go out in public places, any canine droppings must be removed at once. You will always have to carry with you a small plastic bag or "poop-scoop."

Outdoor training includes such surfaces as grass, soil and cement. Indoor training usually means training your dog to newspaper, but this is not a viable option with a large dog like the Cane Corso. When deciding on the surface and location that you will want your Cane Corso to use, be sure that it is going to be permanent. Training your dog to grass and then changing your mind two months later is extremely difficult for both dog and owner.

Next, choose the command you will use each and every time

you want your puppy to relieve himself. "Hurry up" and "Let's go" are examples of commands commonly used by dog owners. Get in the habit of giving the

SAFETY FIRST
While It may seem that the most important things to your dog are eating, sleeping and chewing the upholstery on your furniture, his first concern is actually safety. The domesticated dogs we keep as companions have the same pack instinct as their ancestors who ran free thousands of years ago. Because of this pack instinct, your dog wants to know that he and his pack are not in danger of being harmed, and that his pack has a strong, capable leader. You must establish yourself as the leader early on in your relationship. That way your dog will trust that you will take care of him and the pack, and he will accept your commands without question.

Follow your nose!
It won't take your
Cane pup long to
learn to locate his
relief area.

puppy your chosen relief command before you take him out. That way, when he becomes an adult, you will be able to determine if he wants to go out when you ask him. A confirmation will be signs of interest, such as wagging his tail, watching you intently, going to the door, etc.

PUPPY'S NEEDS

The puppy needs to relieve himself after play periods, after each meal, after he has been sleeping and at any time he indicates that he is looking for a place to urinate or defecate. The urinary and intestinal tract muscles of very young puppies are not fully developed. Therefore, like human babies, puppies need to relieve themselves frequently.

Take your puppy out often—every hour for an eight-week-old, for example—and always immediately after sleeping and eating. The older the puppy, the less often he will need to relieve himself. Finally, as a mature healthy adult, he will require only three to five relief trips per day.

MEALTIME

Mealtime should be a peaceful time for your puppy. Do not put his food and water bowls in a high-traffic area in the house. For example, give him his own little corner of the kitchen where he can eat undisturbed and where he will not be underfoot. Do not allow small children or other family members to disturb the pup when he is eating.

CANINE DEVELOPMENT SCHEDULE

It is important to understand how and at what age a puppy develops into adulthood.
If you are a puppy owner, consult the following Canine Development Schedule to
determine the stage of development your puppy is currently experiencing.
This knowledge will help you as you work with the puppy in the weeks and months ahead.

Period	Age	Characteristics
First to Third	Birth to Seven Weeks	Puppy needs food, sleep and warmth, and responds to simple and gentle touching. Needs mother for security and disciplining. Needs littermates for learning and interacting with other dogs. Pup learns to function within a pack and learns pack order of dominance. Begin socializing pup with adults and children for short periods. Pup begins to become aware of his environment.
Fourth	Eight to Twelve Weeks	Brain is fully developed. Pup needs socializing with outside world. Remove from mother and littermates. Needs to change from canine pack to human pack. Human dominance necessary. Fear period occurs between 8 and 12 weeks. Avoid fright and pain.
Fifth	Thirteen to Sixteen Weeks	Training and formal obedience should begin. Less association with other dogs, more with people, places, situations. Period will pass easily if you remember this is pup's change-to-adolescence time. Be firm and fair. Flight instinct prominent. Permissiveness and over-disciplining can do permanent damage. Praise for good behavior.
Juvenile	Four to Eight Months	Another fear period about 7 to 8 months of age. It passes quickly, but be cautious of fright and pain. Sexual maturity reached. Dominant traits established. Dog should understand sit, down, come and stay by now.

NOTE: THESE ARE APPROXIMATE TIME FRAMES. ALLOW FOR INDIVIDUAL DIFFERENCES IN PUPPIES.

HOUSING

Since the types of housing and control you provide for your puppy have a direct relationship on the success of house-training, we consider the various aspects of both before we begin training. Taking a new puppy home and turning him loose in your house can be compared to turning a child loose in an amusement park and telling the child that the place is all his! The sheer enormity of the place would be too much for him to handle. Instead, offer the puppy clearly defined areas where he can play, sleep, eat and live. A room of the house where the family gathers is the most obvious choice. Puppies are social animals and

TAKE THE LEAD

Do not carry your dog to his relief area. Lead him there on a leash or, better yet, encourage him to follow you to the spot. If you start carrying him to his spot, you might find that your dog won't go to his relief site on his own, and your dog will have the satisfaction of having trained *you*.

need to feel a part of the pack right from the start. Hearing your voice, watching you while you are doing things and smelling you nearby are all positive reinforcers that he is now a member of your pack. Usually a family room, the kitchen or a nearby adjoining breakfast area is

This ten-month-old has learned the routine, and knows when it's time "to go!"

ideal for providing safety and security for both puppy and owner.

Within the designated room, there should be a smaller area that the puppy can call his own. An alcove, a wire or fiberglass dog crate or a partitioned (not boarded!) corner from which he can view the activities of his new family will be fine. The size of the area or crate is the key factor here. The area must be large enough so that the puppy can lie down and stretch out, as well as stand up, without rubbing his head on the top. At the same time, it must be small enough so that he cannot relieve himself at one end and sleep at the other without coming into contact with his droppings. Dogs are, by nature, clean animals and will not remain close to their relief areas unless forced to do so. In those cases, they then become dirty dogs and usually remain that way for life.

The dog's designated area should contain clean bedding and a toy. Water must always be available, in a non-spill container although during house-training you will have to monitor your pup's water intake so you'll know when he needs to go out. During house-training, avoid putting food in the dog's crate, as this will activate the pup's digestive processes and ultimately defeat your purpose.

HOW MANY TIMES A DAY?

AGE	RELIEF TRIPS
To 14 weeks	10
14–22 weeks	8
22–32 weeks	6
Adulthood	4
(dog stops growing)	

These are estimates, of course, but they are a guide to the *minimum* number of opportunities a dog should have each day to relieve himself.

CONTROL

By *control*, we mean helping the puppy to create a lifestyle pattern that will be compatible to that of his human pack (you!). Just as we guide little children to learn our way of life, we must show the puppy when it is time to play, eat, sleep, exercise and even entertain himself.

Your puppy should always sleep in his crate. He should also learn that, during times of household confusion and excessive human activity, such as

HONOR AND OBEY

Dogs are the most honorable animals in existence. They consider another species (humans) as their own. They interface with you. You are their leader. Puppies perceive children to be on their level; their actions around small children are different from their behavior around their adult masters.

can start a fire in the house. If the puppy chews on the arm of the chair when he is alone, you will probably discipline him angrily when you get home. Thus, he makes the association that your coming home means he is going to be punished. (He will not remember chewing the chair and is incapable of making the association of the discipline with his naughty deed.) Accustoming the pup to his designated area not only keeps him safe but also avoids his engaging in destructive behaviors when you are not around.

Times of excitement, such as special occasions, family parties, etc., can be fun for the puppy, providing that he can view the activities from the security of his designated area. He is not underfoot and he is not being fed all sorts of tidbits that will probably cause him stomach distress, yet he still feels a part of the fun.

SCHEDULE

A puppy should be taken to his relief area each time he is released from his designated area, after meals, after play sessions and when he first awakens in the morning (at age eight weeks, this can mean 5 a.m.!). The puppy will indicate that he's ready "to go" by circling or sniffing busily—do not misinterpret these signs. For a puppy less than ten weeks of age, a routine of taking him out every hour is necessary. As the puppy grows, he will be able to

at breakfast when family members are preparing for the day, he can play by himself in relative safety and comfort in his designated area. Each time you leave the puppy alone, he should understand exactly where he is to stay.

Puppies are chewers and cannot tell the difference between things like lamp cords, television wires, shoes, table legs, etc. Chewing into a television wire, for example, can be fatal to the puppy, while a shorted wire

THINK BEFORE YOU BARK

Dogs are sensitive to their masters' moods and emotions. Use your voice wisely when communicating with your dog. Never raise your voice at your dog unless you are trying to correct him. "Barking" at your dog can become as meaningless as "dogspeak" is to you.

wait for longer periods of time

Keep trips to his relief area short. Stay no more than five or six minutes and then return to the house. If he goes during that time, praise him lavishly and take him indoors immediately. If he does not, but he has an accident when you go back indoors, pick him up immediately, say "No! No!" and return to his relief area. Wait a few minutes, then return to the house again. Never hit a puppy or put his face in urine or excrement when he has had an accident!

Once indoors, put the puppy in his crate until you have had time to clean up his accident. Then, release him to the family area and watch him more closely than before. Chances are, his accident was a result of your not picking up his signal or waiting too long before offering him the opportunity to relieve himself. Never hold a grudge against the puppy for accidents.

Let the puppy learn that going outdoors means it is time

to relieve himself, not to play. Once trained, he will be able to play indoors and out and still differentiate between the times for play versus the times for relief. Help him develop regular hours for naps, being alone, playing by himself and just resting, all in his crate. Encourage him to entertain himself while you are busy with your activities. Let him learn that having you near is comforting, but it is not your main purpose in life to provide him with undivided attention. Each time you put your puppy in his own area, use the same command, whatever suits best. Soon he will run to his crate or special area when he hears you say those words.

Crate training provides safety for you, the puppy and the home. It also provides the puppy with a feeling of security, and that helps the puppy achieve self-confidence and clean habits. Remember that one of the primary ingredients in house-

Always clean up after your dog, whether you're in a public place or your own yard.

training your puppy is control. Regardless of your lifestyle, there will always be occasions when you will need to have a place where your dog can stay and be happy and safe. Crate training is the answer for now and in the future.

In conclusion, a few key elements are really all you need for a successful house-training method—consistency, frequency, praise, control and supervision. By following these procedures with a normal, healthy puppy, you and the puppy will soon be

THE SUCCESS METHOD

Success that comes by luck is usually short-lived. Success that comes by well-thought-out proven methods is often more easily achieved and permanent. This is the Success Method. It is designed to give you, the puppy owner, a simple yet proven way to help your puppy develop clean living habits and a feeling of security in his new environment.

6 Steps to Successful Crate Training

1 Tell the puppy "Crate time!" and place him in the crate with a small treat (a piece of cheese or half of a biscuit). Let him stay in the crate for five minutes while you are in the same room. Then release him and praise lavishly. Never release him when he is fussing. Wait until he is quiet before you let him out.

2 Repeat Step 1 several times a day.

3 The next day, place the puppy in the crate as before. Let him stay there for ten minutes. Do this several times.

4 Continue building time in five-minute increments until the puppy stays in his crate for 30 minutes with you in the room. Always take him to his relief area after prolonged periods in his crate.

5 Now go back to Step 1 and let the puppy stay in his crate for five minutes, this time while you are out of the room.

6 Once again, build crate time in five-minute increments with you out of the room. When the puppy will stay willingly in his crate (he may even fall asleep!) for 30 minutes with you out of the room, he will be ready to stay in it for several hours at a time.

past the stage of "accidents" and ready to move on to a clean and rewarding life together.

ROLES OF DISCIPLINE, REWARD AND PUNISHMENT

Discipline, training one to act in accordance with rules, brings order to life. It is as simple as that. Without discipline, particularly in a group society, chaos will reign supreme and the group will eventually perish. Humans and canines are social animals and need some form of discipline in order to function effectively. They must procure food, reproduce to keep their species going and protect their home base and their young. If there were no discipline in the lives of social animals, they would eventually die from starvation and/or predation by other stronger animals. In the case of domestic canines, discipline in their lives is needed in order for them to understand how their pack (you and other family members) functions and how they must act in order to survive.

A large humane society in a

"Pleased to meet you!" Incorporate some fun into your training to keep you both interested and to bring out your Cane's sense of humor.

highly populated area recently surveyed dog owners regarding their satisfaction with their relationships with their dogs. People who had trained their dogs were 75% more satisfied with their pets than those who had never trained their dogs.

Dr. Edward Thorndike, a noted psychologist, established *Thorndike's Theory of Learning*, which states that a behavior that results in a pleasant event tends to be repeated. Furthermore, it concludes that a behavior that results in an unpleasant event tends not to be repeated. It is this theory upon which training methods are based today. For example, if you manipulate a dog

ATTENTION!

Your dog is actually training you at the same time you are training him. Dogs do things to get attention. They usually repeat whatever succeeds in getting your attention.

PRACTICE MAKES PERFECT!

- Have training lessons with your dog every day in several short segments—three to five times a day for a few minutes at a time is ideal.
- Do not have long practice sessions. The dog will become easily bored.
- Never practice when you are tired, ill, worried or in an otherwise negative mood. This will transmit to the dog and may have an adverse effect on his performance.

Think fun, short and above all *positive!* End each session on a high note, rather than a failed exercise, and make sure to give a lot of praise. Enjoy the training and help your dog enjoy it, too.

to perform a specific behavior and reward him for doing it, he is likely to do it again because he enjoyed the end result.

Occasionally, punishment, a penalty inflicted for an offense, is necessary. The best type of punishment often comes from an outside source. For example, a child is told not to touch the stove because he may get burned. He disobeys and touches the stove. In doing so, he receives a burn. From that time on, he respects the heat of the stove and avoids contact with it. Therefore, a behavior that results in an unpleasant event tends not to be repeated.

A good example of a dog's learning the hard way is the dog who chases the house cat. He is told many times to leave the cat alone, yet he persists in teasing the cat. Then, one day, the dog begins chasing the cat but the cat turns and swipes a claw across the dog's face, leaving the dog with a painful gash on his nose. The final result is that the dog stops chasing the cat. Again, a behavior that results in an unpleasant event tends not to be repeated.

TRAINING EQUIPMENT

COLLAR AND LEAD

For a Cane Corso, the collar and lead that you use for training must be one with which you are easily able to work, not too heavy for the dog and perfectly safe.

TREATS

Have a bag of treats on hand; something nutritious and easy to swallow works best. Use a soft treat, a chunk of cheese or a piece of cooked chicken rather than a dry biscuit. By the time the dog has finished chewing a dry treat, he will forget why he is being rewarded in the first place! Incidentally, using food rewards will not teach a dog to beg at the table—the only way to teach a dog to beg at the table is to give him food from the table. In training, rewarding the dog with a food treat will help him associate praise and the treats with learning new behaviors that obviously please his owner.

TRAINING BEGINS: ASK THE DOG A QUESTION

In order to teach your dog anything, you must first get his attention. After all, he cannot learn anything if he is looking away from you with his mind on something else.

To get your dog's attention, ask him "School?" and immediately walk over to him and give him a treat as you tell him "Good dog." Wait a minute or two and repeat the routine, this time with a treat in your hand as you approach within a foot of the dog. Do not go directly to him, but stop about a foot short of him and hold out the treat as you ask "School?" He will see you approaching with a treat in your hand and most likely begin walking toward you. As you meet, give him the treat and praise again.

The third time, ask the question, have a treat in your hand and walk only a short distance toward the dog so that

A sturdy lead, a comfortable collar and of course a tasty treat, and your Cane is ready to go to school.

TRAINING RULES

If you want to be successful in training your dog, you have four rules to obey yourself:
1. Develop an understanding of how a dog thinks.
2. Do not blame the dog for lack of communication.
3. Define your dog's personality and act accordingly.
4. Have patience and be consistent.

that result in positive attention for him.

Remember that the dog does not understand your verbal language; he only recognizes sounds. Your question translates to a series of sounds for him, and those sounds become the signal to go to you and pay attention. The dog learns that if he does this, he will get to interact with you plus receive treats and praise.

THE BASIC COMMANDS

TEACHING SIT

Now that you have the dog's attention, attach his lead and hold it in your left hand, and hold a food treat in your right hand. Place your food hand at the dog's nose and let him lick the treat but not take it from you. Say "Sit" and slowly raise your food hand from in front of the dog's nose up over his head so that he is looking at the ceiling. As he bends his head upward, he will have to bend his knees to maintain his balance. As he bends his knees, he will assume a sit position. At that point, release the food treat and praise lavishly with comments such as "Good dog! Good sit!," etc. Remember to always praise enthusiastically, because dogs relish verbal praise from their owners and feel so proud of themselves whenever they

he must walk almost all the way to you. As he reaches you, give him the treat and praise again.

By this time, the dog will probably be getting the idea that if he pays attention to you, especially when you ask that question, it will pay off in treats and enjoyable activities for him. In other words, he learns that "school" means doing great things with you that are fun and accomplish a behavior.

You will not use food forever in getting the dog to obey your commands. Food is only used to teach new behaviors and, once the dog knows what you want when you give a specific command, you will wean him off the food treats but still maintain the verbal praise. After all, you will always have your voice with you, and there will be many times when you have no food rewards but expect the dog to obey.

Teaching Down

Teaching the down exercise is easy when you understand how the dog perceives the down position, and it is very difficult when you do not. Dogs perceive the down position as a submissive one; therefore, teaching the

down exercise by using a forceful method can sometimes make the dog develop such a fear of the down that he either runs away when you say "Down" or he attempts to snap at the person who tries to force him down.

Have the dog sit close alongside your left leg, facing in the same direction as you are. Hold the lead in your left hand and a food treat in your right. Now place your left hand lightly on the top of the dog's shoulders where they meet above the spinal cord. Do not push down on the dog's shoulders, simply rest your left hand there so you can guide the dog to lie down close to your left leg rather than to swing away from your side when he drops.

Now place the food hand at the dog's nose, say "Down" very softly (almost a whisper) and slowly lower the food hand to the dog's front feet. When the food hand reaches the floor, begin moving it forward along the floor in front of the dog. Keep

Typically, the easiest and first lesson is the sit command. Dogs usually learn this exercise quickly, which is helpful as it serves as a foundation for other commands.

talking softly to the dog, saying things like, "Do you want this treat? You can do this, good dog." Your reassuring tone of voice will help calm the dog as he tries to follow the food in order to get the treat.

When the dog's elbows touch the floor, release the food and praise lavishly. Try to get the dog to maintain that down position for several seconds before you let him sit up again. The goal here is to get the dog to settle down and not feel threatened in the down position.

DOUBLE JEOPARDY

A dog in jeopardy never lies down. He stays alert on his feet because instinct tells him that he may have to run away or fight for his survival. Therefore, if a dog feels threatened or anxious, he will not lie down. Consequently, it is important to keep the dog calm and relaxed as he learns the down exercise.

TEACHING STAY

It is easy to teach the dog to stay in either a sit or down position. Again, we use food and praise during the teaching process as we help the dog to understand exactly what we are expecting him to do.

To teach the sit/stay, start with the dog sitting on your left side as before and hold the lead in your left hand. Have a food treat in your right hand and place your food hand at the dog's nose. Say "Stay" and step out on your right foot to stand directly in front of the dog, toe to toe, as he licks and nibbles the treat. Be sure to keep his head facing upward to maintain the sit position. Count to five and then swing around to stand next to the dog again with him on your left. As soon as you get back to the original position, release the food and praise lavishly.

To teach the down/stay, do the down as previously described. As soon as the dog lies down, say "Stay" and step out on your right foot just as you did in the sit/stay. Count to five and then return to stand beside the dog with him on your left side. Release the treat and praise as always.

Within a week or ten days, you can begin to add a bit of distance between you and your dog when you leave him. When you do, use your left hand open with the palm facing the dog as a stay signal, much the same as the hand signal a police officer uses to stop traffic at an intersection. Hold the food treat in your right hand as before, but this time the food will not be touching the dog's nose. He will watch the food hand and quickly learn that he is going to get that treat as soon as you return to his side.

When you can stand 3 feet away from your dog for 30 seconds, you can then begin building time and distance in both stays. Eventually, the dog can be expected to remain in the stay position for prolonged periods of time until you return to him or call him to you. Always praise lavishly when he stays.

TEACHING COME

If you make teaching "come" an exciting experience, you should never have a student that does not love the game or that fails to come when called. The secret, it seems, is never to teach the word "come."

At times when an owner most wants his dog to come when called, the owner is likely to be upset or anxious and he allows these feelings to come through in the tone of his voice when he calls his dog. Hearing that desperation in his owner's voice, the dog fears the results of going to him and therefore either disobeys outright or runs in the opposite direction. The secret, therefore, is to teach the dog a game and, when you want him to come to you, simply play the

When a treat can't hold your Cane's attention, you know he's had enough! If your dog becomes distracted or disinterested, your training efforts will be futile. Take a break and try again later.

CONSISTENCY PAYS OFF

Dogs need consistency in their feeding schedule, exercise and relief visits, and in the verbal commands you use. If you use "Stay" on Monday and "Stay here, please" on Tuesday, you will confuse your dog. Don't demand perfect behavior during training sessions and then let him have the run of the house the rest of the day. Above all, lavish praise on your pet consistently every time he does something right. The more he feels he is pleasing you, the more willing he will be to learn.

awaiting the dog's success at locating him or her. Once the dog learns to love the game, simply calling out "Where are you?" will bring him running from wherever he is when he hears that all-important question.

The come command is recognized as one of the most important things to teach a dog, but there are trainers who work with thousands of dogs and never use the actual word "come." Yet these dogs will race to respond to a person who uses the dog's name followed by "Where are you?" For example, a woman has a 12-year-old companion dog who went blind, but who never fails to locate her owner when asked, "Where are you?"

Children, in particular, love to play this game with their dogs. Children can hide in smaller places like a shower or bathtub, behind a bed or under a table. The dog needs to work a little bit harder to find these hiding

Your Cane should never fail to come when called as long as you always welcome him with open arms.

game. It is practically a no-fail solution!

To begin, have several members of your family take a few food treats and each go into a different room in the house. Everyone takes turns calling the dog, and each person should celebrate the dog's finding him with a treat and lots of happy praise. When a person calls the dog, he is actually inviting the dog to find him and to get a treat as a reward for "winning."

A few turns of the "Where are you?" game and the dog will understand that everyone is playing the game and that each person has a big celebration

"COME" . . . BACK
Never call your dog to come to you for a correction or scold him when he reaches you. That is the quickest way to turn a come command into "Go away fast!" Dogs think only in the present tense, and your dog will connect the scolding with coming to you, not with the misbehavior of a few moments earlier.

places, but, when he does, he loves to celebrate with a treat and a tussle with a favorite youngster.

TEACHING HEEL

Heeling means that the dog walks beside the owner without pulling. It takes time and patience on the owner's part to succeed at teaching the dog that he (the owner) will not proceed unless the dog is walking calmly beside him. Neither pulling out ahead on the lead nor lagging behind is acceptable.

Begin by holding the lead in your left hand as the dog sits beside your left leg. Move the loop end of the lead to your right hand, but keep your left hand short on the lead so that it keeps the dog in close next to you. Say "Heel" and step forward on your left foot. Keep the dog close to you and take three steps. Stop and have the dog sit next to you in what we now call the heel position. Praise verbally, but do not touch the dog. Hesitate a moment and begin again with "Heel," taking three steps and stopping, at which point the dog is told to sit again.

Your goal here is to have the dog walk those three steps without pulling on the lead. Once he will walk calmly beside you for three steps without pulling, increase the number of steps you take to five. When he will walk politely beside you

while you take five steps, you can increase the length of your walk to ten steps. Keep increasing the length of your stroll until the dog will walk

COMMAND STANCE

Stand up straight and authoritatively when giving your dog commands. Do not issue commands when lying on the floor or lying on your back on the sofa. If you are on your hands and knees when you give a command, your dog will think you are positioning yourself to play.

Attention is essential to success in the show ring, as the dog must be completely focused on the handler and ready to follow directions.

quietly beside you without pulling as long as you want him to heel. When you stop heeling, indicate to the dog that the exercise is over by verbally praising as you pet him and say "OK, good dog." The "OK" is used as a release word, meaning that the exercise is finished and the dog is free to relax.

If you are dealing with a puppy who insists on pulling you around, simply "put on your brakes" and stand your ground until the dog realizes that the two of you are not going anywhere until he is beside you and moving at your pace, not his. It

may take some time just standing there to convince the pup that you are the leader and that you will be the one to decide on the direction and speed of your travel.

Each time the dog looks up at you or slows down to give a slack lead between the two of you, quietly praise him and say "Good heel. Good dog." Eventually, the dog will begin to respond and within a few days he will be walking politely beside you without pulling on the lead. At first, the training sessions should be kept short and very positive; soon the dog will be able to walk nicely with you for increasingly longer distances. Remember also to give the dog free time and the opportunity to run and play when you have finished heel practice.

WEANING OFF FOOD IN TRAINING

Food is used in training new behaviors. Once the dog understands what behavior goes

---

TUG OF WALK?

If you begin teaching the heel by taking long walks and letting the dog pull you along, he misinterprets this action as an acceptable form of taking a walk. When you pull back on the leash to counteract his pulling, he reads that tug as a signal to pull even harder!

with a specific command, it is time to start weaning him off the food treats. At first, give a treat after each exercise. Then, start to give a treat only after every other exercise. Mix up the times when you offer a food reward and the times when you only offer praise so that the dog will never know when he is going to receive both food and praise and when he is going to receive only praise. This is called a variable-ratio reward system. It proves successful because there is always the chance that the owner will produce a treat, so the dog never stops trying for that reward. No matter what, *always* give verbal praise.

OBEDIENCE CLASSES

It is a good idea to enroll in an obedience class if one is available in your area. If yours is a show dog, classes to prepare the two of you for the ring would be more appropriate. Many areas have dog clubs that offer basic obedience training as well as preparatory classes for obedience competition. There are also local dog trainers who offer similar classes.

At dog shows, dogs can earn titles at various levels of competition. The highly trainable Cane certainly can be trained for obedience competition. The beginning levels of obedience competition include basic

HEELING WELL
Teach your dog to heel in an enclosed area. Once you think the dog will obey reliably and you want to attempt advanced obedience exercises such as off-lead heeling, test him in a fenced-in area so he cannot run away.

FETCH!

Play fetching games with your puppy in an enclosed area where he can go for his toy and bring it back to you. Always use a toy or object designated just for this purpose. Never use a shoe, sock or other item he may later confuse with those in your closet or underneath your chair.

behaviors such as sit, down, heel, etc. The more advanced levels of competition include jumping, retrieving, scent discrimination and signal work. The advanced levels require a dog and owner to put a lot of time and effort into their training. The titles that can be earned at these levels of competition are very prestigious.

OTHER ACTIVITIES FOR LIFE

Whether a dog is trained in the structured environment of a class or alone with his owner at home, there are many activities that can bring fun and rewards to both owner and dog once they have mastered basic control.

Teaching the dog to help out around the home, in the yard or on the farm provides great satisfaction to both dog and owner. In addition, the dog's help makes life a little easier for his owner and raises his stature as a valued companion to his family. It helps give the dog a purpose by occupying his mind and providing an outlet for his energy.

Backpacking is an exciting and healthy activity that the dog can be taught without assistance from more than his owner. The exercise of walking and climbing is good for man and dog alike, and the bond that they develop together is priceless. The rule for backpacking with any dog is never to expect the dog to carry more than one-sixth of his body weight.

If you are interested in participating in organized competition with your Cane Corso, there are activities other than obedience in which you and your dog can become involved. Agility is a popular sport in which dogs run through obstacle courses that include various jumps, tunnels and other exercises to test the dog's speed and coordination. The owners run beside their dogs to give commands and to guide them through the course. Although competitive, the focus is on fun—it's fun to do, fun to watch and great exercise. Even though a large breed, the Cane Corso is highly agile, so is capable of success in agility work.

In countries where it is permitted, some Cane Corsi have gained Schutzhund titles; they have also been used in police work. As a Cane Corso owner, you have the opportunity to

Your training efforts will pay off in a Cane Corso who is a wonderful and reliable family companion.

participate in Schutzhund competition if you choose and if it's allowed where you live. Schutzhund originated as a test to determine the best quality German Shepherds to be used for breeding stock, but now it is open to other breeds, too. Breeders continue to use it as a way to evaluate working ability and temperament. There are three levels in Schutzhund trials: SchH. I, SchH. II and SchH. III, with each level being progressively more difficult to complete successfully. Each level consists of training, obedience and protection phases. Training for Schutzhund is intense and must be practiced consistently to keep the dog keen. The experience of Schutzhund training is very rewarding for dog and owner, and the Cane Corso's tractability is well suited for this type of training.

OBEDIENCE TRAINING

Obedience training for Cane Corsi is strongly recommended. This should begin at an early age, and should become a regular part of life. After initial training, lessons do not have to be formal, but personal training with your dog should continue, for this will help your Cane to understand that you are the leader.

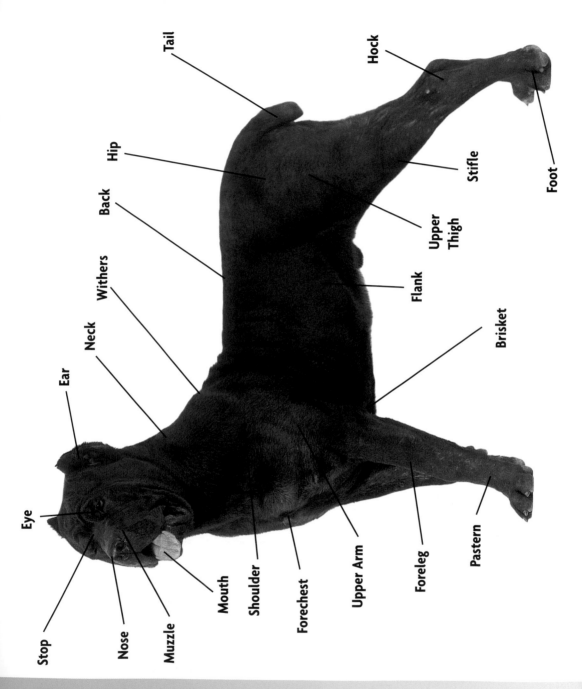

Tail

Hock

Hip

Stifle

Foot

Back

Upper
Thigh

Withers

Flank

Neck

Brisket

Ear

Eye

Mouth

Shoulder

Forechest

Upper Arm

Foreleg

Pastern

Stop

Nose

Muzzle

Physical Structure of the Cane Corso

HEALTH CARE OF YOUR

CANE CORSO

Dogs suffer from many of the same physical illnesses as people and might even share many of the same psychological problems. Since people usually know more about human diseases than canine maladies, many of the terms used in this chapter will be familiar but not necessarily those used by veterinarians. For example, we will use the familiar term *x-ray* instead of *radiograph*. We will also use the familiar term *symptoms*, even though dogs don't have symptoms, which are verbal descriptions of something the patient feels or observes himself that he regards as abnormal. Dogs have *clinical signs* since they cannot speak, so we have to look for these clinical signs...but we still use the term *symptoms* in the book.

Medicine is a constantly changing art, with of course some scientific input as well. Things alter as we learn more and more about basic sciences such as genetics and biochemistry, and have use of more sophisticated imaging techniques like Computer Aided Tomography (CAT scans) or Magnetic Resonance Imaging (MRI scans). There is academic dispute about many canine maladies, so different veterinarians treat them in different ways; for examples, some vets place a greater emphasis on surgical treatments than others.

SELECTING A VETERINARIAN
Your selection of a veterinarian should be based on personal recommendation for his skills with dogs, and, if possible, especially Cane Corsi or similar breeds. If the vet is based nearby, it will be helpful because you might have an emergency or need to make multiple visits for treatments.

All veterinarians are licensed and should be capable of dealing with routine medical issues such as infections, injuries, the promotion of health (for example, by vaccination) and routine surgeries like neutering/spaying, stitching up wounds and the like. If the problem affecting your dog is more complex, your vet will refer your pet to someone with a more detailed knowledge of what

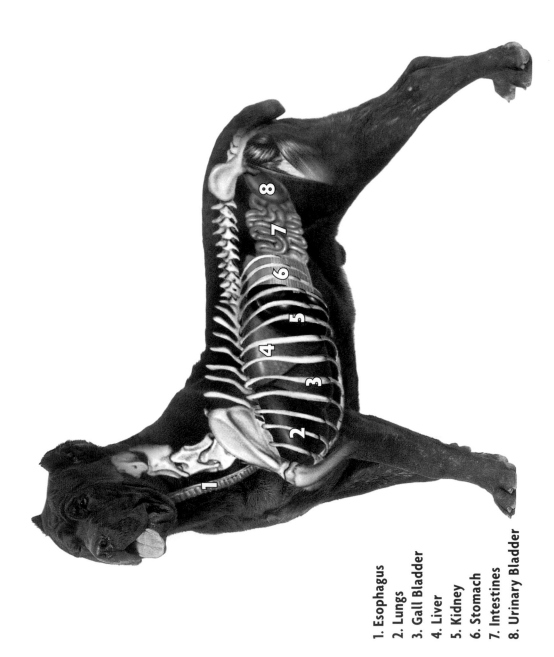

1. Esophagus
2. Lungs
3. Gall Bladder
4. Liver
5. Kidney
6. Stomach
7. Intestines
8. Urinary Bladder

Internal Organs of the Cane Corso

is wrong. This will usually be a specialist, perhaps at the nearest university veterinary school, who concentrates in the field relevant to your dog's problem.

Veterinary procedures are very costly and, as the treatments available improve, they are going to become more expensive. It is quite acceptable to discuss matters of cost with your vet; if there is more than one treatment option, cost may be a factor in deciding which route to take. It also is not impudent to get a second opinion, although it is courteous to advise the vets concerned that you are doing so.

Insurance against veterinary cost is becoming very popular. Depending on the type of coverage you choose, your policy can range from covering emergencies only to including aspects of your dog's routine health care.

PREVENTATIVE MEDICINE

It is much easier, less costly and more effective to practice preventative medicine than to fight bouts of illness and disease. Properly bred puppies of all breeds come from parents that were selected based upon their genetic-disease profiles. The puppies' mother should have been vaccinated, free of all internal and external parasites and properly nourished. For these reasons, a visit to the veterinarian who cared for the dam is recommended if at all

Breakdown of Veterinary Income by Category

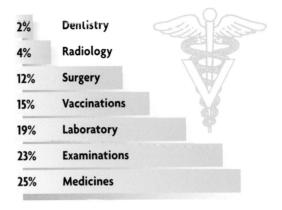

2%	Dentistry
4%	Radiology
12%	Surgery
15%	Vaccinations
19%	Laboratory
23%	Examinations
25%	Medicines

possible. The dam passes disease resistance to her puppies, which should last from eight to ten weeks. Unfortunately, she can also pass on parasites and infection. This is why knowledge about her health is useful in learning more about the health of the puppies.

A typical vet's income, categorized according to services performed. This survey dealt with small-animal (pets) practices.

WEANING TO BRINGING PUPPY HOME
Puppies should be weaned by the time they are two months old. A puppy that remains for at least eight weeks with his mother and littermates usually adapts better to other dogs and people later in life.

Sometimes new owners have their puppy examined by a veterinarian immediately, which is a good idea unless the puppy is overtired by a long journey home from the breeder's. In that case, an appointment should be made for the next day.

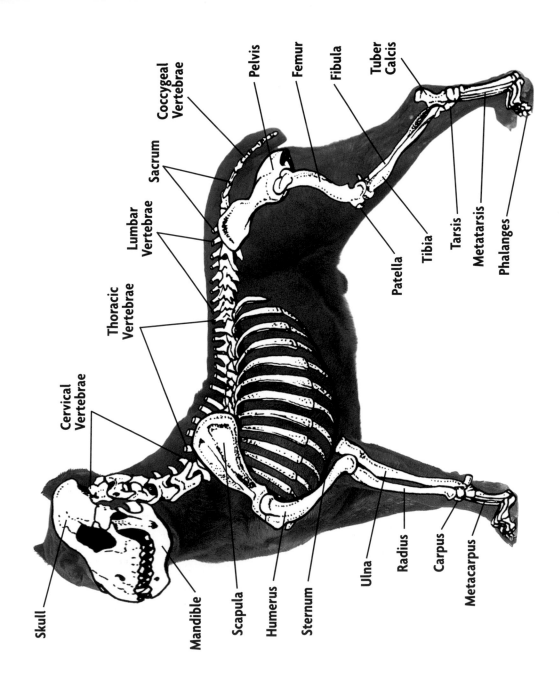

Skeletal Structure of the Cane Corso

Coccygeal Vertebrae

Pelvis

Femur

Fibula

Tuber Calcis

Sacrum

Tarsis

Metatarsis

Phalanges

Lumbar Vertebrae

Tibia

Patella

Thoracic Vertebrae

Cervical Vertebrae

Skull

Mandible

Scapula

Humerus

Sternum

Ulna

Radius

Carpus

Metacarpus

The puppy will have his teeth examined and his skeletal conformation and general health checked prior to certification by the veterinarian. Puppies in certain breeds have problems with their kneecaps, cataracts and other eye problems, heart murmurs and undescended testicles. Your veterinarian might also have training in temperament evaluation. At the first visit, the vet will set up your pup's vaccination schedule.

VACCINATIONS

Most vaccinations are given by injection and should only be given by a veterinarian. Both he and you should keep a record of the date of the injection, the identification of the vaccine and the amount given. Some vets give a first vaccination around six weeks, but most dog breeders prefer the course not to commence until about eight weeks because of the risk of interaction with the antibodies produced by the mother. The vaccination schedule is usually based on a two- to four-week cycle. You must take your vet's advice as to when to vaccinate, as this may differ according to the vaccine used.

HEALTH AND VACCINATION SCHEDULE

AGE IN WEEKS:	6TH	8TH	10TH	12TH	14TH	16TH	20-24TH	52ND
Worm Control	✔	✔	✔	✔	✔	✔	✔	
Neutering							✔	
Heartworm		✔		✔		✔	✔	
Parvovirus	✔		✔		✔		✔	✔
Distemper		✔		✔		✔		✔
Hepatitis		✔		✔		✔		✔
Leptospirosis								✔
Parainfluenza	✔		✔		✔			✔
Dental Examination		✔					✔	✔
Complete Physical		✔					✔	✔
Coronavirus				✔			✔	✔
Canine Cough	✔							
Hip Dysplasia							✔	
Rabies							✔	

Vaccinations are not instantly effective. It takes about two weeks for the dog's immune system to develop antibodies. Most vaccinations require annual booster shots. Your vet should guide you in this regard.

The normal, healthy hairs of a typical dog, enlarged about 200 times normal size. The inset shows the tip of a fine, growing hair about 2,000 times normal size.

The usual vaccines contain immunizing doses of several different viruses such as distemper, parvovirus, parainfluenza and hepatitis. There are other vaccines available when the puppy is at risk. You should rely upon professional advice. This is especially true for the booster immunizations. Most vaccination programs require a booster when the puppy is a year old and once a year thereafter. In some cases, circumstances may require more or less frequent immunizations.

Canine cough, more formally known as tracheobronchitis, is immunized against with a vaccine that is sprayed into the dog's nostrils. Canine cough is usually included in routine vaccination, but it is often not as effective as the vaccines for other major diseases.

FIVE MONTHS TO ONE YEAR OF AGE

Unless you intend to breed or show your dog, neutering the puppy around six months of age is recommended. Discuss this with your veterinarian. Neutering/spaying has proven to

DISEASE REFERENCE CHART

	What is it?	What causes it?	Symptoms
Leptospirosis	Severe disease that affects the internal organs; can be spread to people.	A bacterium, which is often carried by rodents, that enters through mucous membranes and spreads quickly throughout the body.	Range from fever, vomiting and loss of appetite in less severe cases to shock, irreversible kidney damage and possibly death in most severe cases.
Rabies	Potentially deadly virus that infects warm-blooded mammals.	Bite from a carrier of the virus, mainly wild animals.	1st stage: dog exhibits change in behavior, fear. 2nd stage: dog's behavior becomes more aggressive. 3rd stage: loss of coordination, trouble with bodily functions.
Parvovirus	Highly contagious virus, potentially deadly.	Ingestion of the virus, which is usually spread through the feces of infected dogs.	Most common: severe diarrhea. Also vomiting, fatigue, lack of appetite.
Canine cough	Contagious respiratory infection.	Combination of types of bacteria and virus. Most common: *Bordetella bronchiseptica* bacteria and parainfluenza virus.	Chronic cough.
Distemper	Disease primarily affecting respiratory and nervous system.	Virus that is related to the human measles virus.	Mild symptoms such as fever, lack of appetite and mucus secretion progress to evidence of brain damage, "hard pad."
Hepatitis	Virus primarily affecting the liver.	Canine adenovirus type I (CAV-1). Enters system when dog breathes in particles.	Lesser symptoms include listlessness, diarrhea, vomiting. More severe symptoms include "blue-eye" (clumps of virus in eye).
Coronavirus	Virus resulting in digestive problems.	Virus is spread through infected dog's feces.	Stomach upset evidenced by lack of appetite, vomiting, diarrhea.

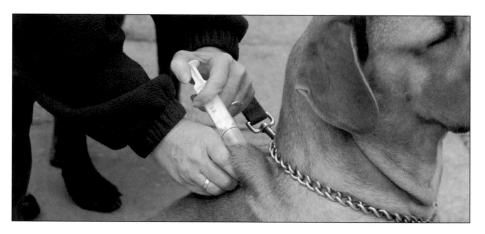

be extremely beneficial to male and female dogs, respectively. Besides eliminating the possibility of pregnancy and pyometra in females and testicular cancer in male dogs, it greatly reduces the risk of (but does not prevent) breast cancer in bitches and prostate cancer in males.

Your veterinarian should provide your puppy with a thorough dental evaluation at six months of age, ascertaining whether all of the permanent teeth have erupted properly. A home dental-care regimen should be initiated at six months, including brushing weekly and providing good dental devices (such as hard plastic or nylon bones). Regular dental care promotes healthy teeth, fresh breath and a longer life.

DOGS OLDER THAN ONE YEAR

Continue to visit the veterinarian at least once a year. There is no

such disease as "old age," but bodily functions do change with age. The eyes and ears are no longer as efficient. Liver, kidney and intestinal functions often decline. Proper dietary changes, recommended by your veterinarian, can make life more pleasant for your aging Cane Corso and you.

SKIN PROBLEMS

Veterinarians are consulted by dog owners for skin problems more than for any other group of diseases or maladies. A dog's skin is as sensitive, if not more so, than human skin, and both can suffer almost the same ailments (though the occurrence of acne in most dogs is rare). For this reason, veterinary dermatology has developed into a specialty practiced by many veterinarians.

Since many skin problems have visual symptoms that are almost identical, it requires the skill of an experienced veterinary dermatologist to identify and cure many of the more severe skin disorders. Pet shops sell many treatments for skin problems, but most of the treatments are directed at symptoms and not at the underlying problem(s). If your dog is suffering from a skin disorder, you should seek professional assistance as quickly as possible. As with all diseases, the earlier a problem is identified and treated, the more likely it is that the cure will be successful.

HEREDITARY SKIN DISORDERS

Veterinary dermatologists are currently researching a number of skin disorders that are believed to have hereditary bases. These inherited diseases are transmitted by both parents, who appear (phenotypically) normal but have a recessive gene for the disease, meaning that they carry, but are not affected by, the disease. These diseases pose serious problems to breeders because in some instances there are no methods of identifying carriers. Often the secondary diseases associated with these skin conditions are even more debilitating than the skin disorders themselves, including cancers and respiratory problems.

Among the hereditary skin disorders, for which the mode of inheritance is known, are acrodermatitis, cutaneous asthenia (Ehlers-Danlos syndrome), sebaceous adenitis, cyclic hematopoiesis, dermatomyositis, IgA deficiency, color dilution alopecia and nodular dermatofibrosis. Some of these disorders are limited to one or two breeds, while others affect a large number of breeds. All inherited diseases must be diagnosed and treated by a veterinary specialist.

PARASITE BITES

Many of us are allergic to insect bites. The bites itch, erupt and may even become infected. Dogs have the same reaction to fleas, ticks and/or mites. When an insect lands on you, you have the chance to whisk it away with your hand. Unfortunately, when a dog is bitten by a flea, tick or mite, he can only scratch it away or bite it. By the time the dog has been bitten, the parasite has done some of its damage. It may also have laid eggs, which will cause further problems in the near future. The itching from parasite bites is probably due to the saliva injected

What's itching your Cane? All dogs enjoy a good scratch now and then, but if the problem persists, it could be a skin problem that requires veterinary attention.

into the site when the parasite sucks the dog's blood.

AIRBORNE ALLERGIES

Just as humans suffer from hay fever during the pollinating season, many dogs suffer from the same allergies. When the pollen count is high, your dog might be affected, but don't expect him to sneeze and have a runny nose as a human would. Dogs react to pollen allergies in the same way they react to fleas—they scratch and bite themselves. Dogs, like humans, can be tested for allergens. Discuss the testing with your veterinarian.

ACRAL LICK GRANULOMA

Many large dogs have a very poorly understood syndrome called acral lick granuloma. The manifestation of the problem is the dog's tireless attack at a specific area of the body, almost always the legs or paws. The dog licks so intensively that he removes the hair and skin, leaving an ugly, large wound. Tiny protuberances, which are outgrowths of new capillaries, bead on the surface of the wound. Owners who notice their dogs' biting and chewing at their extremities should have the vet determine the cause. If lick granuloma is identified, although there is no absolute cure, corticosteroids are the most common treatment.

AUTO-IMMUNE ILLNESSES

An auto-immune illness is one in which the immune system overacts and does not recognize parts of the affected person; rather, the immune system starts to react as if these parts were foreign and need to be destroyed. An example is rheumatoid arthritis, which occurs when the body does not recognize the joints, thus leading to a very painful and damaging reaction in the joints. This has nothing to do with age, so can occur in children and young dogs. The wear-and-tear arthritis of the older person or dog is osteoarthritis.

Lupus is an auto-immune disease that affects dogs as well as people. It can take variable forms, affecting the kidneys, bones and the skin. It usually is treated with steroids, which can themselves have very significant side effects. The steroids calm down the allergic reaction to the body's tissues, which helps the lupus, but they also calm down the body's reaction to real foreign substances such as bacteria as well as thin the skin and bone.

FOOD PROBLEMS

FOOD ALLERGIES

Some dogs can be allergic to many foods that are best-sellers and highly recommended by breeders and veterinarians. Changing the brand of food that you buy may not eliminate the problem if the element to which the dog is allergic is contained in the new brand.

Recognizing a food allergy in a dog can be difficult. Humans often have rashes when we eat foods to which we are allergic, or have swelling of the lips or eyes. Dogs do not usually develop rashes, but react in the same way as they do to an airborne or bite allergy—they itch, scratch and bite. While pollen allergies are usually seasonal, food allergies are year-round problems.

TREATING FOOD ALLERGY

Diagnosis of food allergy is based on a two- to four-week dietary trial with a home-cooked diet fed to the exclusion of all other foods. The diet should consist of boiled rice or potato with a source of protein that the dog has never eaten before, such as fresh or frozen fish, lamb or even

rabbit, venison or pheasant. Water has to be the only drink, and it is really important that no other foods are fed during this trial. If the dog's condition improves, you will need to try the original diet once again to see if the itching resumes. If it does, then this confirms the diagnosis that the dog is allergic to his original diet. The treatment is long-term feeding of something that does not distress the dog's skin, which may be in the form of one of the commercially available hypoaller-genic diets or the home-made diet that you created for the allergy trial.

FOOD INTOLERANCE

Food intolerance is the inability of the dog to completely digest certain foods. This occurs because the dog does not have the chemicals necessary to digest some foodstuffs. These chemicals are called enzymes. All puppies have the enzymes necessary to digest canine milk, but some dogs do not have the enzymes to digest a very different form of milk that is commonly found in human households—milk from cows. In such dogs, drinking cows' milk results in loose bowels, stomach pains and the passage of gas. Dogs often do not have the enzymes to digest soy or other beans. The treatment is to exclude the foodstuffs that upset your Cane Corso's digestion.

A challenge that every dog owner inevitably will face is persuading the dog to take medication. Placing a pill at the back of the dog's mouth and stroking his throat to encourage him to swallow is a tried-and-true technique, although it may take a few tries!

(Left) Cross-section through a Cane Corso, showing how deep the body cavity is. The muscles around the vertebrae give strength to the back.

The cross-section through a Cane Corso shows the muscles around the vertebra.

The abdominal cavity.

(Right) The stomach hangs like a handbag with both straps broken within this deep body cavity. Support is provided by the junction with the esophagus and the junction with the duodenum.

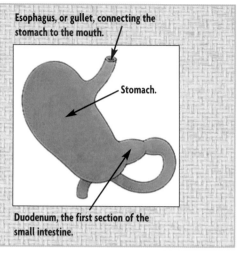

Esophagus, or gullet, connecting the stomach to the mouth.

Stomach.

Duodenum, the first section of the small intestine.

BLOAT OR GASTRIC TORSION

This is a problem found in the large, deep-chested breeds, and is the subject of much research. However, it still manages to take away many dogs before their time and in a very horrible way. By looking at the diagrams, you can see how the stomach can move around easily. Those breeds with the deepest chests are at the greatest risk of having their whole

DETECTING BLOAT

As important as it is to take precautions against bloat/gastric torsion, it is of equal importance to recognize the symptoms. It is necessary for your Cane Corso to get immediate veterinary attention if you notice any of the following signs:

• Your dog's stomach starts to distend, ending up large and as tight as a football;
• Your dog is dribbling, as no saliva can be swallowed;
• Your dog makes frequent attempts to vomit but cannot bring anything up due to the stomach's being closed off;
• Your dog is distressed from pain;
• Your dog starts to suffer from clinical shock, meaning that there is not enough blood in the dog's circulation as the hard, dilated stomach stops the blood from returning to the heart to be pumped around the body. Clinical shock is indicated by pale gums and tongue, as they have been starved of blood. The shocked dog also has glazed, staring eyes.

You have minutes—yes, *minutes*—to get your dog into surgery. If you see any of these symptoms at any time of the day or night, get to the vet immediately. Someone will have to phone and warn that you are on your way (which is a justification for the invention of the cellular phone!), so that they can be prepared to get your pet on the operating table.

HOW TO PREVENT BLOAT

Despite the deep-chested breeds' predisposition to bloat, there are simple daily precautions that you can take to reduce the risk of this condition:
- Feed your dog twice daily rather than offer one big meal;
- Do not exercise your dog for at least one hour before and two hours after he has eaten;
- Make certain that your dog is calm and not overly excited while he is eating. It has been proven that nervous or overly excited dogs are more prone to develop bloat;
- Add a small portion of moist meat product to his dry-food ration;
- Serve his meals in an elevated bowl stand, which avoids the dog's craning his neck while eating and drinking;
- To prevent your dog from gobbling his food too quickly, and thereby swallowing air, put some large (unswallowable) objects into his bowl so that he will have to eat around them to get his food;
- Never allow him to gulp water.

stomachs twist around (gastric torsion). This cuts off the blood supply and prevents the stomach's contents from leaving, thereby increasing the amount of gas in the stomach. Once these things have happened, surgery is vital. If the blood supply has been cut off too long and a bit of the stomach wall dies, death of the Cane Corso is almost inevitable.

The horrendous pain of this condition is due to the stomach wall's being stretched by the gas caught in the stomach, as well as the stomach wall's desperately needing the blood that cannot get to it. There is the pain of not being able to pass a much greater than normal amount of wind; added to this is a pain equivalent to that of a heart attack, which is due to the heart muscle's being starved of blood.

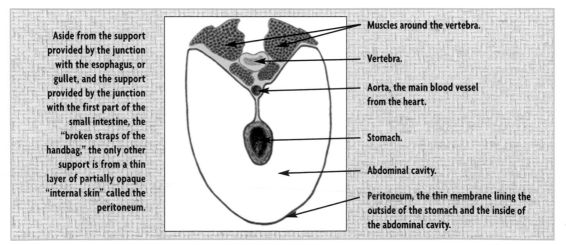

Aside from the support provided by the junction with the esophagus, or gullet, and the support provided by the junction with the first part of the small intestine, the "broken straps of the handbag," the only other support is from a thin layer of partially opaque "internal skin" called the peritoneum.

Muscles around the vertebra.

Vertebra.

Aorta, the main blood vessel from the heart.

Stomach.

Abdominal cavity.

Peritoneum, the thin membrane lining the outside of the stomach and the inside of the abdominal cavity.

A male dog flea, *Ctenocephalides canis.*

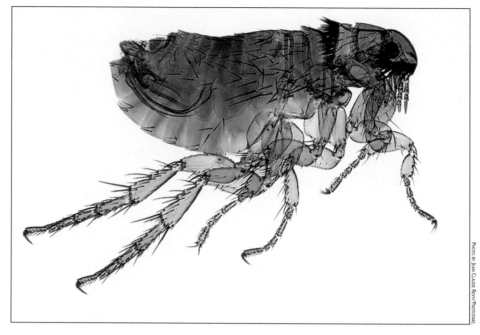

PHOTO BY JEAN CLAUDE REVY/PHOTOTAKE

EXTERNAL PARASITES

FLEAS

Of all the problems to which dogs are prone, none is more well known and frustrating than fleas. Flea infestation is relatively simple to cure but difficult to prevent. Parasites that are harbored inside the body are a bit more difficult to eradicate but they are easier to control.

To control flea infestation, you have to understand the flea's life cycle. Fleas are often thought of as a summertime problem, but centrally heated homes have changed the patterns and fleas can be found at any time of the year. The most effective method of flea control is a two-stage approach: one stage to kill the adult fleas, and the other to control the development of pre-adult fleas. Unfortunately, no single active ingredient is effective against all stages of the life cycle.

FLEA KILLER CAUTION— "POISON"

Flea-killers are poisonous. You should not spray these toxic chemicals on areas of a dog's body that he licks, including his genitals and his face. Flea killers taken internally are a better answer, but check with your vet in case internal therapy is not advised for your dog.

LIFE CYCLE STAGES

During its life, a flea will pass through four life stages: egg, larva, pupa or nymph and adult. The adult stage is the most visible and irritating stage of the flea life cycle, and this is why the majority of flea-control products concentrate on this stage. The fact is that adult fleas account for only 1% of the total flea population, and the other 99% exist in pre-adult stages, i.e., eggs, larvae and nymphs. The pre-adult stages are barely visible to the naked eye.

THE LIFE CYCLE OF THE FLEA

Eggs are laid on the dog, usually in quantities of about 20 or 30, several times a day. The adult female flea must have a blood meal before each egg-laying session. When first laid, the eggs will cling to the dog's hair, as the eggs are still moist. However, they will quickly dry out and fall from the dog, especially if the dog moves around or scratches. Many eggs will fall off in the dog's favorite area or an area in which he spends a lot of time, such as his bed.

Once the eggs fall from the dog onto the carpet or furniture, they will hatch into larvae. This takes from one to ten days. Larvae are not particularly mobile and will usually travel only a few inches from where they hatch. However, they do have a tendency to move away from bright light and heavy

EN GARDE:
CATCHING FLEAS OFF GUARD!
Consider the following ways to arm yourself against fleas:
- Add a small amount of pennyroyal or eucalyptus oil to your dog's bath. These natural remedies repel fleas.
- Supplement your dog's food with fresh garlic (minced or grated) and a hearty amount of brewer's yeast, both of which ward off fleas.
- Use a flea comb on your dog daily. Submerge fleas in a cup of bleach to kill them quickly.
- Confine the dog to only a few rooms to limit the spread of fleas in the home.
- Vacuum daily...and get all of the crevices! Dispose of the bag every few days until the problem is under control.
- Wash your dog's bedding daily. Cover cushions where your dog sleeps with towels, and wash the towels often.

traffic—under furniture and behind doors are common places to find high quantities of flea larvae.

The flea larvae feed on dead organic matter, including adult flea feces, until they are ready to change into adult fleas. Fleas will usually remain as larvae for around seven days. After this period, the larvae will pupate into protective pupae. While inside the pupae, the larvae will undergo metamorphosis and change into adult fleas. This can take as little time as a few days, but the adult fleas can remain inside the pupae waiting to hatch for up to two years. The pupae are signaled to hatch by certain stimuli, such as physical pressure—the pupae's being stepped on, heat from an animal's lying on the pupae or increased carbon-dioxide levels and vibrations—indicating that a suitable host is available.

Once hatched, the adult flea must feed within a few days. Once the adult flea finds a host, it will not leave voluntarily. It only becomes dislodged by grooming or the host animal's scratching. The adult flea will remain on the

PHOTO BY DWIGHT R. KUHN

host for the duration of its life unless forcibly removed.

TREATING THE ENVIRONMENT AND THE DOG

Treating fleas should be a two-pronged attack. First, the environment needs to be treated; this includes carpets and furniture, especially the dog's bedding and areas underneath furniture. The environment should be treated with a household spray containing an Insect Growth Regulator (IGR) and an insecticide to kill the adult fleas. Most IGRs are effective against eggs and larvae; they actually mimic the fleas' own hormones and stop the eggs and larvae from developing into adult fleas. There are currently no treatments available to attack the pupa stage of the life cycle, so the adult insecticide is used to kill the newly hatched adult fleas before they find a host. Most IGRs are active for many months, while adult insecticides are only active

A scanning electron micrograph of a dog or cat flea, *Ctenocephalides*, magnified more than 100x. This image has been colorized for effect.

S. E. M. BY DR DENNIS KUNKEL, UNIVERSITY OF HAWAII.

THE LIFE CYCLE OF THE FLEA

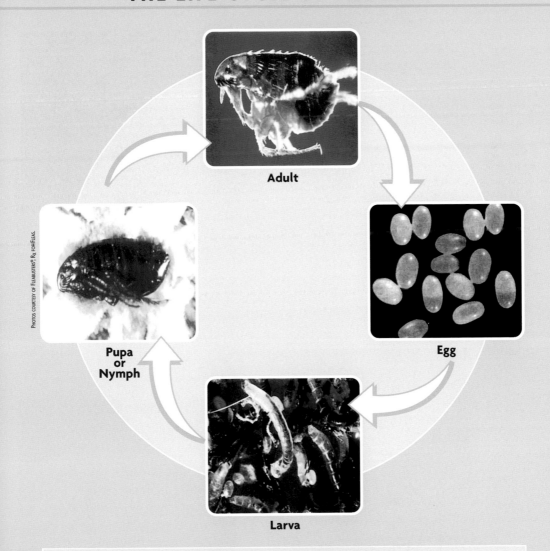

Adult

Egg

Larva

Pupa or Nymph

Fleas have been around for millions of years and have adapted to changing host animals. They are able to go through a complete life cycle in less than one month or they can extend their lives to almost two years by remaining as pupae or cocoons. They do not need blood or any other food for up to 20 months.

INSECT GROWTH REGULATOR (IGR)

Two types of products should be used when treating fleas—a product to treat the pet and a product to treat the home. Adult fleas represent less than 1% of the flea population. The pre-adult fleas (eggs, larvae and pupae) represent more than 99% of the flea population and are found in the environment; it is in the case of pre-adult fleas that products containing an Insect Growth Regulator (IGR) should be used in the home.

IGRs are a new class of compounds used to prevent the development of insects. They do not kill the insect outright, but instead use the insect's biology against it to stop it from completing its growth. Products that contain methoprene are the world's first and leading IGRs. Used to control fleas and other insects, this type of IGR will stop flea larvae from developing and protect the house for up to seven months.

for a few days.

When treating with a house-hold spray, it is a good idea to vacuum before applying the product. This stimulates as many pupae as possible to hatch into adult fleas. The vacuum cleaner should also be treated with an insecticide to prevent the eggs and larvae that have been collected in the vacuum bag from hatching.

The second stage of treatment is to apply an adult insecticide to the dog. Traditionally, this would be in the form of a collar or a spray, but more recent innovations include digestible insecticides that poison the fleas when they ingest the dog's blood. Alternatively, there are drops that, when placed on the back of the dog's neck, spread throughout the hair and skin to kill adult fleas.

TICKS

Though not as common as fleas, ticks are found all over the tropical and temperate world. They don't bite, like fleas; they harpoon. They dig their sharp proboscis (nose) into the dog's skin and drink the blood. Their only food and drink is dog's

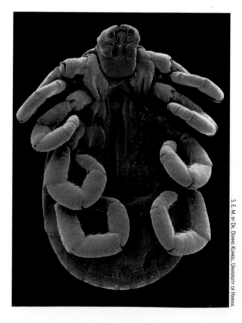

S. E. M. BY DR. DENNIS KUNKEL, UNIVERSITY OF HAWAII

blood. Dogs can get Lyme disease, Rocky Mountain spotted fever, tick bite paralysis and many other diseases from ticks. They may live where fleas are found and they like to hide in cracks or seams in walls. They are controlled the same way fleas are controlled.

The American dog tick, *Dermacentor variabilis*, may well be the most common dog tick in many geographical areas, especially those areas where the climate is hot and humid. Most dog ticks have life expectancies of a week to six months, depending upon climatic conditions. They can neither jump nor fly, but they can crawl slowly and can range up to 16 feet to reach a sleeping or unsuspecting dog.

MITES
Just as fleas and ticks can be problematic for your dog, mites can also lead to an itchy nuisance. Microscopic in size, mites are related to ticks and generally take up permanent residence on their host animal—in this case, your dog! The term *mange* refers to any infestation caused by one of the mighty mites, of which there are six varieties that concern dog owners.

Demodex mites cause a condition known as demodicosis (sometimes called red mange or

DEER-TICK CROSSING
The great outdoors may be fun for your dog, but it also is a home to dangerous ticks. Deer ticks carry a bacterium known as *Borrelia burgdorferi* and are most active in the autumn and spring. When infections are caught early, penicillin and tetracycline are effective antibiotics, but, if left untreated, the bacteria may cause neurological, kidney and cardiac problems as well as long-term trouble with walking and painful joints.

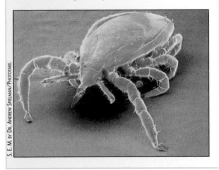

S. E. M. BY DR. ANDREW SPIELMAN/PHOTOTAKE.

PHOTO BY DR. DENNIS KUNKEL, UNIVERSITY OF HAWAII.

The head of an American dog tick, *Dermacentor variabilis*, enlarged and colorized for effect.

PHOTO BY JAMES HAYDEN/YOAV/PHOTOTAKE.

follicular mange), in which the mites live in the dog's hair follicles and sebaceous glands in larger-than-normal numbers. This type of mange is commonly passed from the dam to her puppies and usually shows up on the puppies' muzzles, though demodicosis is not transferable from one normal dog to another. Most dogs recover from this type of mange without any treatment, though topical therapies are commonly prescribed by the vet.

The *Cheyletiellosis* mite is the hook-mouthed culprit associated with "walking dandruff," a condition that affects dogs as well as cats and rabbits. This mite lives on the surface of the animal's skin and is readily transferable through direct or indirect contact with an affected animal. The dandruff is present in the form of scaly skin, which may or may not be itchy. If not treated, this mange can affect a whole kennel of dogs and can be spread to humans as well.

The *Sarcoptes* mite causes intense itching on the dog in the form of a condition known as scabies or sarcoptic mange. The cycle of the *Sarcoptes* mite lasts about three weeks, and the mites live in the top layer of the dog's skin (epidermis), preferably in areas with little hair. Scabies is highly contagious and can be passed to humans. Sometimes an allergic reaction to the mite worsens the severe itching associated with sarcoptic mange.

Ear mites, *Otodectes cynotis,* lead to otodectic mange, which most commonly affects the outer ear canal of the dog, though other areas can be affected as well. Dogs with ear-mite infestation commonly scratch at their ears, causing further irritation, and shake their heads. Dark brown droppings in the outer ear confirm the diagnosis. Your vet can prescribe a treatment to flush out the ears and kill any eggs in the ears. A complete month of treatment is necessary to cure the mange.

Two other mites, less common in dogs, include *Dermanyssus gallinae* (the poultry or red mite) and *Eutrombicula alfreddugesi* (the North American mite associated with trombiculidiasis or chigger infestation). The poultry mite frequently lives on chickens, but can transfer to dogs who spend time near farm animals. Chigger infestation affects dogs in the

DO NOT MIX

Never mix parasite-control products without first consulting your vet. Some products can become toxic when combined with others and can cause fatal consequences.

NOT A DROP TO DRINK

Never allow your dog to swim in polluted water or public areas where water quality can be suspect. Even perfectly clear water can harbor parasites, many of which can cause serious to fatal illnesses in canines. Areas inhabited by waterfowl and other wildlife are especially dangerous.

central US who have exposure to woodlands. The types of mange caused by both of these mites are treatable by vets.

INTERNAL PARASITES

Most animals—fishes, birds and mammals, including dogs and humans—have worms and other parasites that live inside their bodies. According to Dr. Herbert R. Axelrod, the fish pathologist, there are two kinds of parasites: dumb and smart. The smart parasites live in peaceful cooperation with their hosts (symbiosis), while the dumb parasites kill their hosts. Most worm infections are relatively easy to control. If they are not controlled, they weaken the host dog to the point that other medical problems occur, but they do not kill the host as dumb parasites would.

A brown dog tick, *Rhipicephalus sanguineus*, is an uncommon but annoying tick found on dogs.

PHOTO BY CAROLINA BIOLOGICAL SUPPLY/PHOTOTAKE.

Photo by Carolina Biological Supply/Phototake.

The roundworm *Rhabditis* can infect both dogs and humans.

ROUNDWORMS

Average-size dogs can pass 1,360,000 roundworm eggs every day. For example, if there were only 1 million dogs in the world, the world would be saturated with thousands of tons of dog feces. These feces would contain around 15,000,000,000 roundworm eggs.

Up to 31% of home yards and children's sand boxes in the US contain roundworm eggs.

Flushing dog's feces down the toilet is not a safe practice because the usual sewage treatments do not destroy roundworm eggs.

Infected puppies start shedding roundworm eggs at three weeks of age. They can be infected by their mother's milk.

The roundworm, *Ascaris lumbricoides*.

Photo by Dwight R. Kuhn.

ROUNDWORMS

The roundworms that infect dogs are known scientifically as *Toxocara canis*. They live in the dog's intestines and shed eggs continually. It has been estimated that a dog produces about 6 or more ounces of feces every day. Each ounce of feces averages hundreds of thousands of roundworm eggs. There are no known areas in which dogs roam that do not contain roundworm eggs. The greatest danger of roundworms is that they infect people, too! It is wise to have your dog tested regularly for round-worms.

In young puppies, round-worms cause bloated bellies, diarrhea, coughing and vomiting, and are transmitted from the dam (through blood or milk). Affected puppies will not appear as animated as normal puppies. The worms appear spaghetti-like, measuring as long as 6 inches. Adult dogs can acquire round-worms through coprophagia (eating contaminated feces) or by killing rodents that carry round-worms.

Roundworm infection can kill puppies and cause severe problems in adults, as the hatched larvae travel to the lungs and trachea through the bloodstream. Cleanliness is the best preventative for roundworms. Always pick up after your dog and dispose of feces in appropriate receptacles.

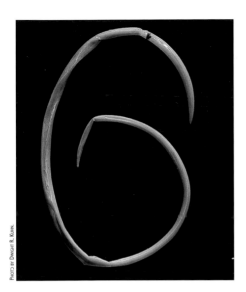

PHOTO BY DWIGHT R. KUHN.

HOOKWORMS

In the United States, dog owners have to be concerned about four different species of hookworm, the most common and most serious of which is *Ancylostoma caninum*, which prefers warm climates. The others are *Ancylostoma braziliense*, *Ancylostoma tubaeforme* and *Uncinaria stenocephala,* the latter of which is a concern to dogs living in the northern US and Canada, as this species prefers cold climates.

Hookworms are dangerous to humans as well as to dogs and cats, and can be the cause of severe anemia due to iron deficiency. The worm uses its teeth to attach itself to the dog's intestines and changes the site of its attachment about six times per day. Each time the worm reposi-

tions itself, the dog loses blood and can become anemic. *Ancylostoma caninum* is the most likely of the four species to cause anemia in the dog.

Symptoms of hookworm infection include dark stools, weight loss, general weakness, pale coloration and anemia, as well as possible skin problems. Fortunately, hookworms are easily purged from the affected dog with a number of medications that have proven effective. Discuss these with your vet. Most heartworm preventatives include a hookworm insecticide as well.

Owners also must be aware that hookworms can infect humans, who can acquire the larvae through exposure to contaminated feces. Since the worms cannot complete their life cycle on a human, the worms simply infest the skin and cause irritation. This condition is known as cutaneous larva migrans syndrome. As a preventative, use disposable gloves or a "poop-scoop" to pick up your dog's droppings and prevent your dog (or neighborhood cats) from defecating in children's play areas.

The hookworm, *Ancylostoma caninum.*

PHOTO BY C. JAMES WEBB/PHOTOTAKE.

The infective stage of the hookworm larva.

TAPEWORMS

Humans, rats, squirrels, foxes, coyotes, wolves and domestic dogs are all susceptible to tapeworm infection. Except in humans, tapeworms are usually not a fatal infection. Infected individuals can harbor 1000 parasitic worms.

Tapeworms, like some other types of worm, are hermaphroditic, meaning male and female in the same worm.

If dogs eat infected rats or mice, or anything else infected with tapeworm, they get the tapeworm disease. One month after attaching to a dog's intestine, the worm starts shedding eggs. These eggs are infective immediately. Infective eggs can live for a few months without a host animal.

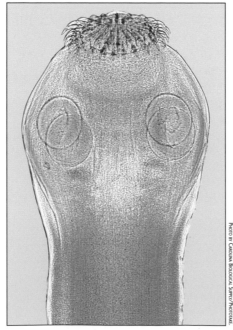

The head and rostellum (the round prominence on the scolex) of a tapeworm, which infects dogs and humans.

PHOTO BY CAROLINA BIOLOGICAL SUPPLY/PHOTOTAKE.

TAPEWORMS

There are many species of tapeworm, all of which are carried by fleas! The most common tapeworm affecting dogs is known as *Dipylidium caninum*. The dog eats the flea and starts the tapeworm cycle. Humans can also be infected with tapeworms—so don't eat fleas! Fleas are so small that your dog could pass them onto your hands, your plate or your food and thus make it possible for you to ingest a flea that is carrying tapeworm eggs.

While tapeworm infection is not life-threatening in dogs (smart parasite!), it can be the cause of a very serious liver disease for humans. About 50% of the humans infected with *Echinococcus multilocularis*, a type of tapeworm that causes alveolar hydatid, perish.

WHIPWORMS

In North America, whipworms are counted among the most common parasitic worms in dogs. The whipworm's scientific name is *Trichuris vulpis*. These worms attach themselves in the lower parts of the intestine, where they feed. Affected dogs may only experience upset tummies, colic and diarrhea. These worms, however, can live for months or years in the dog, beginning their larval stage in the small intestine, spending their adult stage in the large intestine and finally passing infective eggs through the dog's feces. The only way to detect whipworms is through a fecal examination, though this is not always foolproof. Treatment for whipworms is tricky, due to the worms' unusual life-cycle pattern, and very often dogs are reinfected due to exposure to infective eggs on the ground. The whipworm eggs can survive in the environment for as long as five years; thus, cleaning up droppings in your own backyard as well as in public places is absolutely essential for sanitation purposes and the health of your dog and others.

THREADWORMS

Though less common than roundworms, hookworms and those previously mentioned, threadworms concern dog owners in the southwestern US and Gulf Coast area where the climate is hot and humid. Living in the small intestine of the dog, this worm measures a mere 2 millimeters and is round in shape. Like that of the whipworm, the threadworm's life cycle is very complex and the eggs and larvae are passed through the feces. A deadly disease in humans, *Strongyloides* readily infects people, and the handling of feces is the most common means of transmission. Threadworms are most often seen in young puppies; bloody diarrhea and pneumonia are symptoms. Sick puppies must be isolated and treated immediately; vets recommend a follow-up treatment one month later.

HEARTWORM PREVENTATIVES

There are many heartworm preventatives on the market, many of which are sold at your veterinarian's office. These products can be given daily or monthly, depending on the manufacturer's instructions. All of these preventatives contain chemical insecticides directed at killing heartworms, which leads to some controversy among dog owners. In effect, heartworm preventatives are necessary evils, though you should determine how necessary based on your pet's lifestyle. There is no doubt that heartworm is a dreadful disease that threatens the lives of dogs. However, the likelihood of your dog's being bitten by an infected mosquito is slim in most places, and a mosquito-repellent (or an herbal remedy such as Wormwood or Black Walnut) is much safer for your dog and will not compromise his immune system (the way heartworm preventatives will). Should you decide to use the traditional preventative "medications," you can consider giving the pill every other or third month. Since the toxins in the pill will kill the heartworms at all stages of development, the pill would be effective in killing larvae, nymphs or adults, and it takes four months for the larvae to reach the adult stage. Thus, there is no rationale to poisoning the dog's system on a monthly basis. Lastly, do not give the pill during the winter months since there are no mosquitoes around to pass on their infection, unless you live in a tropical environment.

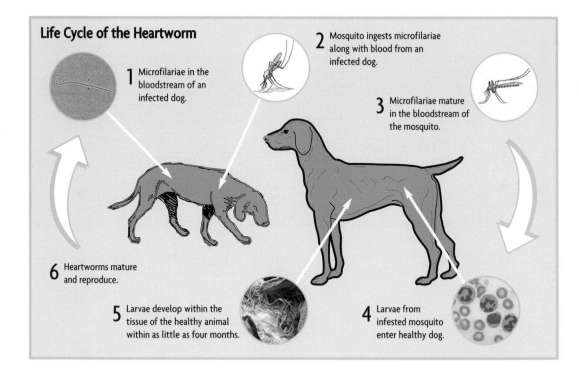

Life Cycle of the Heartworm

1 Microfilariae in the bloodstream of an infected dog.

2 Mosquito ingests microfilariae along with blood from an infected dog.

3 Microfilariae mature in the bloodstream of the mosquito.

6 Heartworms mature and reproduce.

5 Larvae develop within the tissue of the healthy animal within as little as four months.

4 Larvae from infested mosquito enter healthy dog.

HEARTWORMS

Heartworms are thin, extended worms up to 12 inches long, which live in a dog's heart and the major blood vessels surrounding it. Dogs may have up to 200 worms. Symptoms may be loss of energy, loss of appetite, coughing, the development of a pot belly and anemia.

Heartworms are transmitted by mosquitoes. The mosquito drinks the blood of an infected dog and takes in larvae with the blood. The larvae, called microfilariae, develop within the body of the mosquito and are passed on to the next dog bitten after the larvae mature. It takes two to three weeks for the larvae to develop to the infective stage within the body of the mosquito. Dogs are usually treated at about six weeks of age and maintained on a prophylactic dose given monthly.

Blood testing for heartworms is not necessarily indicative of how seriously your dog is infected. Although this is a dangerous disease, it is not easy for a dog to be infected. Discuss the various preventatives with your vet, as there are many different types now available. Together you can decide on a safe course of prevention for your dog.

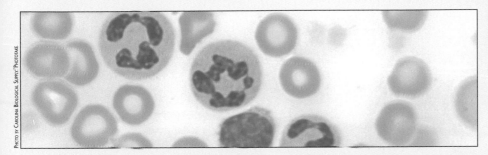

Magnified
heartworm larvae,
Dirofilaria immitis.

PHOTO BY CAROLINA BIOLOGICAL SUPPLY/PHOTOTAKE

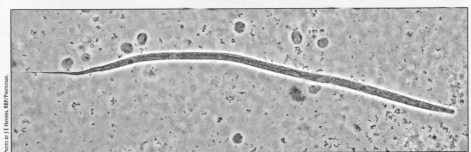

Heartworm,
*Dirofilaria
immitis.*

PHOTO BY J E HAYDEN, RBP/PHOTOTAKE.

The heart
of a dog infected
with canine
heartworm,
*Dirofilaria
immitis.*

PHOTO BY JAMES E. HAYDEN, RBP/PHOTOTAKE.

HOMEOPATHY:
an alternative
to conventional
medicine

"Less is Most"

Using this principle, the strength of a homeopathic remedy is measured by the number of serial dilutions that were undertaken to create it. The greater the number of serial dilutions, the greater the strength of the homeopathic remedy. The potency of a remedy that has been made by making a dilution of 1 part in 100 parts (or 1/100) is 1c or 1cH. If this remedy is subjected to a series of further dilutions, each one being 1/100, a more dilute and stronger remedy is produced. If the remedy is diluted in this way six times, it is called 6c or 6cH. A dilution of 6c is 1 part in 1,000,000,000,000. In general, higher potencies in more frequent doses are better for acute symptoms and lower potencies in more infrequent doses are more useful for chronic, long-standing problems.

CURING OUR DOGS NATURALLY

Holistic medicine means treating the whole animal as a unique, perfect, living being. Generally, holistic treatments do not suppress the symptoms that the body naturally produces, as do most medications prescribed by conventional doctors and vets. Holistic methods seek to cure disease by regaining balance and harmony in the patient's environment. Some of these methods include use of nutritional therapy, herbs, flower essences, aromatherapy, acupuncture, massage, chiropractic and, of course, the most popular holistic approach, homeopathy.

Homeopathy is a theory or system of treating illness with small doses of substances which, if administered in larger quantities, would produce the symptoms that the patient already has. This approach is often described as "like cures like." Although modern veterinary medicine is geared toward the "quick fix," homeopathy relies on the belief that, given the time, the body is able to heal itself and return to its natural, healthy state.

Choosing a remedy to cure a problem in our dogs is the difficult part of homeopathy. Consult with your vet for a professional diagnosis of your dog's symptoms. Often these symptoms require

immediate conventional care. If your vet is willing and knowledgeable, you may attempt a homeopathic remedy. Be aware that cortisone prevents homeopathic remedies from working. There are hundreds of possibilities and combinations to cure many problems in dogs, from basic physical problems such as excessive shedding, fleas or other parasites, unattractive doggy odor, bad breath, upset tummy, obesity, dry, oily or dull coat, diarrhea, ear problems or eye discharge (including tears and dry or mucousy matter), to behavioral abnormalities such as fear of loud noises, habitual licking, poor appetite, excessive barking and various phobias. From alumina to zincum metallicum, the remedies span the planet and the imagination...from flowers and weeds to chemicals, insect droppings, diesel smoke and volcanic ash.

Using "Like to Treat Like"

Unlike conventional medicines that suppress symptoms, homeopathic remedies treat illnesses with small doses of substances that, if administered in larger quantities, would produce the symptoms that the patient already has. While the same homeopathic remedy can be used to treat different symptoms in different dogs, here are some interesting remedies and their uses.

Apis Mellifica
(made from honey bee venom) can be used for allergies or to reduce swelling that occurs in acutely infected kidneys.

Diesel Smoke
can be used to help control travel sickness.

Calcarea Fluorica
(made from calcium fluoride, which helps harden bone structure) can be useful in treating hard lumps in tissues.

Natrum Muriaticum
(made from common salt, sodium chloride) is useful in treating thin, thirsty dogs.

Nitricum Acidum
(made from nitric acid) is used for symptoms you would expect to see from contact with acids, such as lesions, especially where the skin joins the linings of body orifices or openings such as the lips and nostrils.

Symphytum
(made from the herb Knitbone, *Symphytum officinale*) is used to encourage bones to heal.

Urtica Urens
(made from the common stinging nettle) is used in treating painful, irritating rashes.

Number-One Killer Disease in Dogs: CANCER

In every age, there is a word associated with a disease or plague that causes humans to shudder. In the 21st century, that word is "cancer." Just as cancer is the leading cause of death in humans, it claims nearly half the lives of dogs that die from a natural disease as well as half the dogs that die over the age of ten years.

Described as a genetic disease, cancer becomes a greater risk as the dog ages. Vets and dog owners have become increasingly aware of the threat of cancer to dogs. Statistics reveal that one dog in every five will develop cancer, the most common of which is skin cancer. Many cancers, including prostate, ovarian and breast cancer, can be avoided by spaying and neutering our dogs by the age of six months.

Early detection of cancer can save or extend a dog's life, so it is absolutely vital for owners to have their dogs examined by a qualified vet or oncologist immediately upon detection of any abnormality. Certain dietary guidelines have also proven to reduce the onset and spread of cancer. Foods based on fish rather than beef, due to the presence of Omega-3 fatty acids, are recommended. Other amino acids such as glutamine have significant benefits for canines, particularly those breeds that show a greater susceptibility to cancer.

Cancer management and treatments promise hope for future generations of canines. Since the disease is genetic, breeders should never breed a dog whose parents, grandparents and any related siblings have developed cancer. It is difficult to know whether to exclude an otherwise healthy dog from a breeding program, as the disease does not manifest itself until the dog's senior years.

RECOGNIZE CANCER WARNING SIGNS

Since early detection can possibly rescue your dog from becoming a cancer statistic, it is essential for owners to recognize the possible signs and seek the assistance of a qualified professional.

- Abnormal bumps or lumps that continue to grow
- Bleeding or discharge from any body cavity
- Persistent stiffness or lameness
- Recurrent sores or sores that do not heal
- Inappetence
- Breathing difficulties
- Weight loss
- Bad breath or odors
- General malaise and fatigue
- Eating and swallowing problems
- Difficulty urinating and defecating

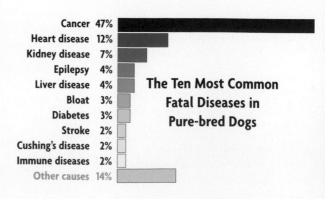

Cancer	47%
Heart disease	12%
Kidney disease	7%
Epilepsy	4%
Liver disease	4%
Bloat	3%
Diabetes	3%
Stroke	2%
Cushing's disease	2%
Immune diseases	2%
Other causes	14%

The Ten Most Common Fatal Diseases in Pure-bred Dogs

CDS: COGNITIVE DYSFUNCTION SYNDROME
"Old-Dog Syndrome"

There are many ways for you to evaluate old-dog syndrome. Veterinarians have defined CDS (cognitive dysfunction syndrome) as the gradual deterioration of cognitive abilities. These are indicated by changes in the dog's behavior. When a dog changes his routine response, and maladies have been eliminated as the cause of these behavioral changes, then CDS is the usual diagnosis.

More than half the dogs over eight years old suffer from some form of CDS. The older the dog, the more chance he has of suffering from CDS. In humans, doctors often dismiss the CDS behavioral changes as part of "winding down."

There are four major signs of CDS: frequent potty accidents inside the home, sleeping much more or much less than normal, acting confused and failing to respond to social stimuli.

SYMPTOMS OF CDS

FREQUENT POTTY ACCIDENTS
- *Urinates in the house.*
- *Defecates in the house.*
- *Doesn't signal that he wants to go out.*

SLEEP PATTERNS
- *Awakens more slowly.*
- *Sleeps more than normal during the day.*
- *Sleeps less during the night.*

CONFUSION
- *Goes outside and just stands there.*
- *Appears confused with a faraway look in his eyes.*
- *Hides more often.*
- *Doesn't recognize friends.*
- *Doesn't come when called.*
- *Walks around listlessly and without a destination.*

FAILURE TO RESPOND TO SOCIAL STIMULI
- *Comes to people less frequently, whether called or not.*
- *Doesn't tolerate petting for more than a short time.*
- *Doesn't come to the door when you return home.*

SHOWING YOUR
CANE CORSO

When you purchase your Cane Corso, you will make it clear to the breeder whether you want one just as an able protector and pet, or if you hope to be buying a Cane Corso with show prospects. No reputable breeder will sell you a young puppy and tell you that it is *definitely* of show quality, for so much can go wrong during the early months of a puppy's development. If you plan to show, what you will hopefully have acquired is a puppy with "show potential."

To the novice, exhibiting a

The Cane Corso has an impressive presence in the show ring.

Cane Corso in the show ring may look easy, but it takes a lot of hard work and devotion to do top winning at shows, not to mention a little luck too!

SHOWING BASICS
The first concept that the canine novice learns when watching a dog show is that each dog first competes against members of his own breed. Once the judge has selected the best member of each breed (Best of Breed), provided that the show is judged on a Group system, that chosen dog will compete with other dogs in his group. Finally, the dogs chosen first in each group will compete for Best in Show.

The second concept that you must understand is that the dogs are not actually compared against one another. The judge compares each dog against the breed standard set forth for that particular breed. The standard is the written description of the ideal specimen that is approved by the governing kennel club. While some early breed standards were indeed based on specific dogs that were famous or popular, many dedicated enthusiasts say that a perfect specimen, as described in the standard, has never walked into a show ring, has never been bred and, to the woe of dog breeders around the globe, does not exist. Breeders attempt to get as close to this

CLUB CONTACTS
You can get information about dog shows from the national kennel clubs:

Fédération Cynologique Internationale
14, rue Leopold II, B-6530
Thuin, Belgium
www.fci.be

American Rare Breed Association
9921 Frank Tippett Road
Cheltenham, MD 20623
www.arba.org

International Cane Corso Federation
www.canecorso.org

Italian Kennel Club
ENCI (Ente Nazionale della Cinofilia Italiana)
Viale Corsica 20
20137 Milan, Italy
www.enci.it

Società Amatori Cane Corso
Via Flli Cervi, 1
37047 San Bonaficia (VR), Italy

Cane Corso Preservation Society
www.canecorsoitaliano.org

ideal as possible with every litter, but theoretically the "perfect" dog is so elusive that it is impossible. (And if the "perfect" dog were born, breeders and judges would never agree that it was indeed "perfect.")

If you are interested in exploring the world of dog showing, your best bet is to join your local breed club or the country's national parent club for the Cane Corso. These clubs often host both regional and national specialties, shows only for Cane Corsi, which can

The Cane Corso breed ring. As the dogs line up, "stacked" to show themselves off in the best possible manner, the judge reviews all of the entries while mentally comparing them to the ideal dog described in the breed standard.

include conformation competition as well as performance events. Even if you have no intention of competing with your Cane Corso, a specialty is like a festival for lovers of the breed who congregate to share their favorite topic: the Cane Corso! Clubs also send out newsletters, and some organize training days and seminars in order that people may learn more about their chosen breed. To locate the breed club closest to you, contact the parent club or the organization with which your dog is registered, which furnishes the rules and regulations for all of these events.

Kennel clubs and breed clubs can also give you information about dog shows in your area in which the Cane Corso would be eligible to compete. Provided

that your Cane Corso does not have a disqualifying fault, he can compete in conformation showing. Only unaltered dogs can be entered in a dog show, so if you have spayed or neutered your Cane Corso, your dog cannot compete in conformation shows. The reason for this is simple. Dog shows are the main forum to prove which representatives of a breed are worthy of

TEMPERAMENT PLUS
Although it seems that physical conformation is the only factor considered in the show ring, temperament is also of utmost importance. An aggressive or fearful dog should not be shown, as bad behavior will not be tolerated and may pose a threat to the judge, other exhibitors, you and your dog.

being bred. Only dogs that have achieved championships—the "seal of approval" for quality in pure-bred dogs—should be bred. Altered dogs, however, can participate in other events such as obedience and other performance trials, and canine good citizen programs.

Before you actually step into the ring, you would be well advised to sit back and observe the judge's ring procedure. If it is your first time in the ring, do not be over-anxious and run to the front of the line. It is much better to stand back and study how the exhibitor in front of you is performing. The judge asks each handler to stand (or "stack") the dog, hopefully showing the dog off to his best advantage. The judge will observe the dog from a distance and from different angles, and approach the dog to check his teeth, overall structure, alertness and muscle tone, as well as consider how well the dog "conforms" to the standard. Most importantly, the judge will have the exhibitor move the dog around the ring in some pattern that he should specify (another advantage to not going first, but always listen since some judges change their directions—and the judge is always right!). Finally, the judge will give the dog one last look before moving on to the next exhibitor.

If you are not in the top four

An example of a quality breed representative at a show in the Netherlands.

in your class at your first show, do not be discouraged. Be patient and consistent, and you may eventually find yourself in a winning line-up. Remember that the winners were once in your shoes and have devoted many hours and much money to earn the placement. If you find that your dog is losing every time and never getting a nod, it may be time to consider a different dog sport or to just enjoy your Cane

Corso as a pet. Parent clubs offer other events, such as agility, tracking, obedience, instinct tests and more, which may be of interest to the owner of a well-trained Cane Corso.

FÉDÉRATION CYNOLOGIQUE INTERNATIONALE

Established in 1911, the Fédération Cynologique Internationale (FCI) represents the "world kennel club." This international body brings uniformity to the breeding, judging and showing of pure-bred dogs. Although the FCI originally included only five European nations: France, Germany, Austria, the Netherlands and Belgium (which remains its headquarters), the organization today embraces nations on six continents and recognizes well over 300 breeds of pure-bred dog.

The FCI sponsors both

Two Cane Corsi patiently await their turn in the ring in the benching area at the World Dog Show.

FCI INFORMATION
There are 330 breeds recognized by the FCI, and each breed is considered to be "owned" by a specific country. Each breed standard is a cooperative effort between the breed's country and the FCI's Standards and Scientific Commissions. Judges use these official breed standards at shows held in FCI member countries. One of the functions of the FCI is to update and translate the breed standards into French, English, Spanish and German.

national and international shows. The hosting country determines the judging system and breed standards are always based on the breed's country of origin. Dogs from every country can participate in these impressive canine spectacles, the largest of which is the World Dog Show, hosted in a different country each year.

There are three titles attainable through the FCI: the International Champion, which is the most prestigious; the International Beauty Champion, which is based on aptitude certificates in different countries; and the International Trial Champion, which is based on achievement in obedience trials in different countries. An FCI title requires a dog to win three CACs (*Certificats d'Aptitude au Championnat*) at

All dogs, regardless of breed, must be gaited in the show ring so that the judge can evaluate movement and structure.

regional or club shows under three different judges who are breed specialists. The title of International Champion is gained by winning four CACIBs (*Certificats d'Aptitude au Championnat International de Beauté*), which are offered only at international shows, with at least a one-year lapse between the first and fourth award.

The FCI is divided into ten groups, in which the recognized breeds are classified. The Cane Corso competes in Group 2 for Molossians. At the World Dog Show, the following classes are offered for each breed: Puppy Class (6–9 months), Junior Class (9–18 months), Open Class (15 months or older) and Champion Class. A dog can be awarded a classification of Excellent, Very Good, Good, Sufficient and Not Sufficient. Puppies can be awarded classifications of Very Promising, Promising or Not Promising. Four placements are made in each class. After all of the classes are judged, a Best of Breed is selected. Other special groups and classes may also be shown. Each exhibitor showing a dog receives a written evaluation from the judge.

Besides the World Dog Show, the European Champions Show and other all-breed shows, you can exhibit your dog at specialty shows held by different breed clubs. Specialty shows may have their own regulations.

BEHAVIOR OF YOUR
CANE CORSO

As a Cane Corso owner, you have selected your dog so that you and your loved ones can have a companion, a protector, a friend and a four-legged family member. You invest time, money and effort to care for and train the family's new charge. Of course, this chosen canine behaves perfectly! Well, perfectly like a *dog*.

THINK LIKE A DOG
Dogs do not think like humans, nor do humans think like dogs, though we try. Unfortunately, a dog is incapable of comprehending how humans think, so the responsibility falls on the owner to adopt a viable canine mindset. Dogs cannot rationalize, and they exist in the present moment. Many a dog owner makes the mistake in training of thinking that he can reprimand his dog for something the dog did a while ago. Basically, you cannot even reprimand a dog for something he did 20 seconds ago! Either catch him in the act or forget it! It is a waste of your and your dog's time—in his mind, you are reprimanding him for whatever he is doing at that moment.

The following behavioral problems represent some that

owners most commonly encounter. Every dog is unique and every situation is unique. No author could purport for you to solve your Cane Corso's problems simply by reading a chapter. Here we outline some basic "dogspeak" so that owners' chances of solving behavioral problems are increased.

Discuss bad habits with your veterinarian and he can recommend a behavioral specialist to consult in appropriate cases. Since behavioral abnormalities are the main reason for owners' abandoning their pets, we hope that you will make a valiant effort to solve your Cane Corso's problems. Patience and understanding are virtues that must dwell in every pet-loving household.

AGGRESSION
Aggression is seen most commonly in breeds with fighting or protection backgrounds, so owners of the Cane Corso must position themselves sensibly to handle aggression in their powerful canine pals. Aggression can be a very big problem in dogs, and, when not controlled, always becomes dangerous. An aggressive dog, no matter the size, may lunge

at, bite or even attack a person or another dog. Aggressive behavior is not to be tolerated and can lead to serious injury. It is painful for a family to watch their dog become unpredictable in his behavior to the point where they are afraid of him. While not all aggressive behavior is dangerous, things like growling, baring teeth, etc. can be frightening. It is important to ascertain why the dog is acting in this manner. Aggression is a display of dominance, and the dog should not have the dominant role in his pack, which is, in this case, your family.

It is important not to challenge an aggressive dog, as this could provoke an attack. Observe your Cane Corso's body language. Does he make direct eye contact and stare? Does he try to make himself as large as possible: ears pricked, chest out, tail erect? Height and size signify authority in a dog pack—being taller or "above" another dog literally means that he is "above" in social status. These body signals tell you that your Cane Corso thinks he is in charge, a problem that needs to be addressed right away. An aggressive dog is unpredictable; you never know when he is going to strike and what he is going to do. You cannot understand why a dog that is playful one minute is growling the next.

Fear is a common cause of aggression in dogs. Perhaps your

NO BUTTS ABOUT IT!
Dogs get to know each other by sniffing each other's backsides. It seems that each dog has a telltale odor, probably created by the anal glands. It also distinguishes sex and signals when a female will be receptive to a male's attention. Some dogs snap at another dog's intrusion of their private parts.

Cane Corso had a negative experience as a puppy, which causes him to be fearful when a similar situation presents itself later in life. The dog may act aggressively in order to protect himself from whatever is making him afraid. It is not always easy to determine what is making your dog fearful, but if you can isolate what brings out the fear reaction, you can help the dog overcome it.

Supervise your Cane Corso's interactions with people in different situations, and praise the dog when it goes well. If he starts to act aggressively in a situation, correct him and remove him from the situation. Do not let people approach the dog and start petting him without your express permission. That way, you can have the dog sit to accept petting, and praise him when he behaves properly. You are focusing on praise and on modifying his behavior by rewarding him when he acts appropriately. By being gentle and by supervising his interactions, you are showing him that there is no need to be afraid or defensive.

A dog's body language tells more than words can say. Exposing the belly is a submissive posture, and not one that all dogs feel comfortable in. This dog's rolling over for a tummy rub says that he completely trusts his owner.

The best solution is to consult a behavioral specialist, one who has experience with the Cane Corso or similar breeds if possible. Together, perhaps you can pinpoint the cause of your dog's aggression and do something about it. An aggressive dog cannot be trusted, and a dog that cannot be trusted is not safe to have as a family pet. If, very unusually, you find that your pet has become untrustworthy and you feel it necessary to seek a new home with a more suitable family and environment, you must explain fully to the new owners all of your reasons for rehoming the dog to be fair to all concerned and for their safety.

AGGRESSION TOWARD OTHER DOGS
A dog's aggressive behavior toward another dog stems from not enough exposure to other dogs at an early age. Coupled with this is the fact that the Cane Corso is naturally dog-aggressive and dominant toward other dogs. While he will not look for a fight, he will stand his ground when instigated; this is a large, powerful breed that will not back down. Furthermore, upon reaching maturity, both sexes are likely to become intolerant of other dogs, males especially so, which is why early socialization is so essential in this breed.

If other dogs make your Cane Corso nervous and agitated, he

will lash out as a protective mechanism. A dog that has not received sufficient exposure to other canines tends to think that he is the only dog on the planet. The animal becomes so dominant that he does not even show signs that he is fearful or threatened. Without growling or any other physical signal as a warning, he will lunge at and bite the other dog.

It is essential that owners of the Cane Corso accept the breed's natural dominant and aggressive tendencies and act responsibly. Keep your Cane away from strange dogs and always supervise any interactions with friends' dogs. If you have socialized your Cane properly, you should be able to trust him with other dogs whom he knows.

DOMINANT AGGRESSION

A social hierarchy is firmly established in a wild dog pack. The dog wants to dominate those under him and please those above him. Dogs know that there must be a leader. If you are not the obvious choice for emperor, the dog will assume the throne! These conflicting innate desires are what a dog owner is up against when he sets about training a dog. In training a dog to obey commands, the owner is reinforcing that he is the top dog in the pack and that the dog should, and should want to, serve his superior. Thus, the owner is suppressing the dog's urge to dominate by modifying his behavior and making him obedient. In the Cane Corso, males tend to be more dominant than females and more likely to challenge their owners for leadership.

An important part of training is taking every opportunity to reinforce that you are the leader. The simple action of making your Cane sit to wait for his food instead of allowing him to run up to get it when he wants it says that you control when he eats; he is dependent on you for food.

Although it may be difficult, do not give in to your dog's wishes every time he whines at you or looks at you with pleading eyes. It is a constant effort to show the dog that his place in the pack is at the bottom. This is not meant to sound cruel or inhumane. You love your Cane and you should treat him with care and affection. Dog training is not about being cruel, it is about molding the dog's behavior into what is acceptable and teaching him to live by your rules.

In theory, it is quite simple: catch him in appropriate behavior and reward him for it. Add a dog into the equation and it becomes a bit more trying but, as a rule of thumb, positive reinforcement is what works best. With a dominant dog, punishment and negative reinforcement can have the opposite effect of what you are after. It can make a dog fearful and/or act out aggressively if he feels he is being challenged. Remember, a dominant dog perceives himself at the top of the social heap and will fight to defend his perceived status. The best way to prevent that is to never give him reason to think that he is in control in the first place.

If you are having trouble training your Cane Corso and it seems as if he is constantly challenging your authority, seek the help of an obedience trainer or behavioral specialist. A professional will work with both you and your dog to teach you effective techniques to use at home. Beware of trainers who rely on excessively harsh methods; scolding is necessary now and then, but the focus in your training should *always* be on positive reinforcement.

I'M HOME!

Dogs left alone for varying lengths of time may often react wildly when their owners return. Sometimes they run, jump, bite, chew, tear things apart, wet themselves, gobble their food or behave in very undisciplined ways. If your dog behaves in this manner upon your return home, allow him to calm down before greeting him or he will consider your attention as a reward for his antics.

SEPARATION ANXIETY

Recognized by behaviorists as the most common form of stress for dogs, separation anxiety can also lead to destructive behaviors in your dog. It's more than your Cane's howling his displeasure at your leaving the house and his being left alone. This is a normal reaction, no different than the child who cries as his mother leaves him on the first day at school. Separation anxiety is more serious. In fact, if you are constantly with your dog, he will come to expect you with him all of the time, making it even more traumatic for him when you are not there.

Obviously, you enjoy spending time with your dog, and he thrives on your love and attention. However, it should not become a dependent relationship in which he is heartbroken without you. This broken heart can also bring on destructive behavior as well as loss of appetite, depression and lack of interest in play and interaction. Canine behaviorists have been spending much time and energy to help owners better understand the significance of this stressful condition.

One thing you can do to minimize separation anxiety is to make your entrances and exits as low-key as possible. Do not give your dog a long drawn-out good-bye, and do not lavish him with hugs and kisses when you return.

This is giving in to the attention that he craves, and it will only make him miss it more when you are away. Another thing you can try is to give your dog a treat when you leave; this will not only keep him occupied and keep his mind off the fact that you have just left, but it will also help him associate your leaving with a pleasant experience.

You may have to accustom your dog to being left alone in intervals. Of course, when your dog starts whimpering as you approach the door, your first instinct will be to run to him and comfort him. Do not do it! Eventually he will adjust to your absence. His anxiety stems from being placed in an unfamiliar situation; by familiarizing him with being alone, he will learn that he will survive. That is not to say you should purposely leave your dog home alone, but the dog needs to know that, while he can depend on you for his care, you do not have to be by his side 24 hours a day. Some behaviorists recommend tiring the dog out before you leave home—take him for a good long walk or engage him in a game of fetch in the yard.

When the dog is alone in the house, he should be placed in his crate—another distinct advantage to crate training your dog. The crate should be placed in his familiar happy family area, where he normally sleeps and already

feels comfortable, thereby making him feel more at ease when he is alone. Be sure to give the dog a special chew toy to enjoy while he settles into his crate.

SEXUAL BEHAVIOR

Dogs exhibit certain sexual behaviors that may have influenced your choice of male or female when you first purchased your Cane Corso. To a certain extent, spaying/neutering will eliminate these behaviors, but if you are purchasing a dog that you wish to breed from, you should be aware of what you will have to deal with throughout the dog's life.

Female dogs usually have two estruses per year, with each season lasting about three weeks. These are the only times in which

Cane Corsi sincerely thrive on interaction with their owners. If your dog spends time alone during the day, be sure to include him in the family's activities when you are at home.

a female dog will mate, and she usually will not allow this until the second week of the cycle, although this varies from bitch to bitch. If not bred during the heat cycle, it is not uncommon for a bitch to experience a false pregnancy, in which her mammary glands swell and she exhibits maternal tendencies toward toys or other objects.

With male dogs, owners must be aware that whole dogs (dogs who are not neutered) have the natural inclination to mark their territory. Males mark their territory by spraying small amounts of urine as they lift their legs in a macho ritual. Marking can occur both outdoors in the yard and around the neighborhood as well as indoors on furniture legs, curtains and the sofa. Such behavior can be very frustrating for the

owner; early training is strongly urged before the "urge" strikes your dog. Neutering the male at an appropriate early age can solve this problem before it becomes a habit.

Other problems associated with males are wandering and mounting. Both of these habits, of course, belong to the unneutered dog, whose sexual drive leads him away from home in search of the bitch in heat. Males will mount females in heat, as well as any other dog, male or female, that happens to catch their fancy. Other possible mounting partners include his owner, the furniture, guests to the home and strangers on the street. Discourage such behavior early on.

Owners must further recognize that mounting is not merely a sexual expression but also one of dominance, seen in males and females alike. Be consistent and be persistent, and you will find that you can "move mounters."

CHEWING

The national canine pastime is chewing! Every dog loves to sink his "canines" into a tasty bone, so it is important to provide your dog with appropriate chew toys so that he doesn't destroy your possessions or chew on dangerous objects. Dogs need to chew to massage their gums, to make their new teeth feel better and to exercise their jaws. This is a natural

Strong jaws need strong toys! The Cane Corso is easily capable of causing much damage if he chews on your belongings, so be sure to keep his mind and teeth occupied with an array of safe, interesting toys.

behavior that is deeply embedded in all things canine.

Our role as owners is not to stop the dog's chewing, but rather to redirect it to positive, chew-worthy objects. Be an informed owner and purchase proper chew toys, like strong nylon bones that will not splinter. This is especially important with the strong-jawed Cane; he will need the most indestructible chews available. Be sure that the objects are safe and durable, and remove toys that have become broken or worn, since your dog's safety is at risk. Again, the owner is responsible for ensuring a dog-proof environment.

It is also the owner's responsibility to provide the dog with sufficient exercise and activity. Some Cane resort to chewing when bored; once they get going, they certainly can cause a lot of damage.

The best answer is prevention; that is, put your shoes, handbags and other tasty objects in their proper places (out of the reach of the growing canine mouth). Direct your puppy to his toys whenever you see him "tasting" the furniture legs or the leg of your trousers. Make a loud noise to attract the pup's attention and immediately escort him to his chew toy and engage him with the toy for at least four minutes, praising and encouraging him all the while. An array of safe, interesting chew toys will keep your dog's mind and teeth occupied, and distracted from chewing on things he shouldn't.

Some trainers recommend deterrents, such as hot pepper, a bitter spice or a product designed for this purpose, to discourage the dog from chewing unwanted objects. Test these products with your own dog to see which works best before investing in large quantities.

JUMPING UP
Jumping up is a dog's friendly way of saying hello! Some dog owners do not mind when their dog jumps up. The problem arises when guests come to the house and the dog greets them in the same manner—whether they like it or not! However friendly the greeting may be, the chances are that your visitors will not appreciate 100 pounds of Cane Corso leaping at them in an enthusiastic greeting, especially if the greeting ends up with someone's unintentionally being knocked to the ground. The dog will not be able to distinguish upon whom he can jump and whom he cannot. Therefore, it is probably best to discourage this behavior entirely.

Pick a command such as "Off" (avoid using "Down" since you will use that for the dog to lie down) and tell him "Off" when he jumps up. Place him on the ground on all fours and have him

sit, praising him the whole time. Always lavish him with praise and petting when he is in the sit position. In this way, you can give him a warm affectionate greeting, let him know that you are as excited to see him as he is to see you and instill good manners at the same time!

DIGGING

Digging, which is seen as a destructive behavior to humans, is actually quite a natural behavior in dogs. Although terriers (the "earth dogs") are most associated with digging, any dog's desire to dig can be irrepressible and most frustrating to his owners. When digging occurs in your yard, it is actually a normal behavior redirected into something the dog can do in his everyday life. In the wild, a dog would be actively seeking food, making his own shelter, etc. He would be using his paws in a purposeful manner for his survival. Since you provide him with food and shelter, he has no need to use his paws for these purposes, and so the energy that he would be using may manifest itself in the form of little holes all over your yard and flowerbeds.

Perhaps your dog is digging as a reaction to boredom—it is somewhat similar to someone eating a whole bag of chips in front of the TV—because they are there and there is nothing better to do! Basically, the answer is to provide the dog with adequate play and exercise so that his mind and paws are occupied, and so that he feels as if he is doing something useful.

Of course, digging is easiest to control if it is stopped as soon as possible, but it is often hard to catch a dog in the act. If your dog is a compulsive digger and is not easily distracted by other activities, you can designate an area on your property where he is allowed to dig. If you catch him digging in an off-limits area of the yard, immediately take him to the approved area and praise him for digging there. Keep a close eye on him so that you can catch him in the act— that is the only way to make him understand what is permitted and what is not. If you take him to a hole he dug an hour ago and tell him "No," he will understand that you are not fond of holes, dirt or flowers. If you catch him while he is stifle-deep in your tulips, that is when he will get your message.

BARKING

Dogs cannot talk—oh, what they would say if they could! Instead, barking is a dog's way of "talking." It can be somewhat frustrating because it is not always easy to tell what a dog means by his bark—is he excited, happy, frightened or angry? Whatever it is that the dog is trying to say, he should not be punished for barking. It is only when the barking becomes excessive, and when the excessive barking becomes a bad habit, that the behavior needs to be modified.

Fortunately, the Cane Corso is generally a quiet animal, but will bark when alerted to a strange noise or situation. If an intruder came into your home in the middle of the night and your Cane barked a warning, wouldn't you be pleased? You would probably deem your dog a hero, a wonderful guardian and protector of the home. On the other hand, if a friend drops by unexpectedly, rings the doorbell and is greeted with a sudden sharp bark, you would probably be annoyed at the dog. But in reality, isn't this just the same behavior? The dog does not know any better. Unless he sees who is at the door and it is

someone he knows, he will bark as a means of vocalizing that his (and your) territory is being threatened. While your friend is not posing a threat, it is all the same to the dog. Barking is his means of letting you know that there is an intrusion, whether friend or foe, on your property. This type of barking is instinctive and should not be discouraged.

Excessive habitual barking, however, is a problem that should be corrected early on. As your Cane grows up, you will be able to tell when his barking is purposeful and when it is for no reason. You will become able to distinguish your dog's different barks and their meanings. For example, the bark when someone comes to the door will be different than the bark when he is excited to see you. It is similar to a person's tone of voice, except that the dog has to rely totally on tone of voice because he does not have the benefit of using words. An incessant barker will be evident at an early age.

There are some things that encourage a dog to bark. For example, if your dog barks non-stop for a few minutes and you give him a treat to quiet him, he believes that you are rewarding him for barking. He will associate barking with getting a treat and will keep doing it until he is rewarded. On the other hand, if

Food stealing is a challenging game with a tasty reward! Eliminate temptation by keeping food where the dog cannot reach it, see it or smell it!

you give him a command such as "Quiet" and praise him after he has stopped barking for a few seconds, he will get the idea that being "quiet" is what you want him to do.

FOOD STEALING

Is your dog devising ways of stealing food from your breakfast table or kitchen counter? If so, you must answer the following questions: Is your Cane Corso a bit hungry, or is he "constantly famished" like many dogs seem to be? Face it, some dogs are more food-motivated than others. They are totally obsessed by the smell of food and can only think of their next meal. Food stealing is terrific fun and always yields a great reward— food, glorious food!

Your goal as an owner, therefore, is to be sensible about where food is placed in the home and to reprimand your dog whenever he is caught in the act of stealing. But remember, only reprimand your dog if you actually see him stealing, not later when the crime is discovered; that will be of no use at all and will only serve to confuse him.

BEGGING

Just like food stealing, begging is a favorite pastime of hungry puppies! It achieves that same great result—*food!* Dogs quickly learn that their owners keep the "good food" for ourselves, and that we humans do not dine on dry food alone. Begging is a conditioned response related to a specific stimulus, time and place. The sounds of the kitchen, cans and bottles opening, crinkling bags, the smell of food in preparation, etc., will excite the dog, and soon the paws will be in the air!

Here is the solution to stopping this behavior: Never give in to a beggar! You are rewarding the dog for sitting pretty, jumping up, whining and rubbing his nose into you by giving him food. By ignoring the dog, you will (eventually) force the behavior into extinction. Note that the behavior is likely to get worse before it disappears, so be sure there are not any "softies" in the family who will give in to "Olivero" every time he whimpers, "More, please."

COPROPHAGIA

Feces eating is, to humans, one of the most disgusting behaviors that their dogs could engage in; yet, to dogs, it is perfectly normal. It is hard for us to understand why a dog would want to eat his own feces. Some possible reasons are that he could be seeking certain nutrients that are missing from his diet, he could be just hungry or he could be attracted by the pleasing (to a dog) scent. While coprophagia most often refers to the dog's eating his own feces, a dog may just as likely eat that of another animal as well if he comes across it. Dogs often find the stool of cats and horses more palatable than that of other dogs.

Vets have found that diets with low levels of digestibility, containing relatively low levels of fiber and high levels of starch, increase coprophagia. Therefore, high-fiber diets may decrease the likelihood of dogs' eating feces. Both the consistency of the stool (how firm it feels in the dog's mouth) and the presence of undigested nutrients may increase the likelihood.

To discourage this behavior, first make sure that the food you are feeding your dog is nutritionally complete and that he is getting enough food. Cane eat a lot, as befits their Italian heritage. If changes in his diet do not seem to work, and no medical cause can be found, you will have to modify the behavior through environmental control before it becomes a habit. The best way to prevent your dog from eating his stool is to make it unavailable—clean up after he eliminates and remove any stool from the yard. Keep your cat's litter box clean at all times.

Reprimanding for stool eating rarely impresses the dog. Vets recommend distracting the dog while he is in the act of stool eating. Coprophagia is seen most frequently in pups 6 to 12 months of age, and usually disappears around the dog's first birthday.

INDEX